Wuthe Heights

--A Study Guide

By Francis Gilbert

This edition first published in 2015 by FGI publishing:
www.francisgilbert.co.uk;
fgipublishing.com
Copyright © 2015 Francis Gilbert
FGI Publishing, London UK, sir@francisgilbert.co.uk

ISBN-13: 978-1519156983

ISBN-10: 1519156987

Dedication
To my sister: Suzie.

Acknowledgments
First, huge thanks must go to my wife, Erica Wagner, for always supporting me with my writing and teaching. Second, I'm very grateful to all the students, teachers, lecturers and other lively people who have helped me write this book.
Also by Francis Gilbert:
I'm A Teacher, Get Me Out Of Here (2004)
Teacher On The Run (2005)
Yob Nation (2006)
Parent Power (2007)
Working The System: How To Get The Very State Education For Your Child (2011)
The Last Day Of Term (2012)
Gilbert's Study Guides on: *Frankenstein, Far From The Madding Crowd, The Hound of the Baskervilles, Pride and Prejudice, The Strange Case of Dr Jekyll and Mr Hyde, The Turn of the Screw, Wuthering Heights* (2013)
Dr Jekyll & Mr Hyde: The Study Guide Edition (2014)
Romeo and Juliet: The Study Guide Edition (2014)
Charlotte Brontë's Jane Eyre: The Study Guide Edition (2015)
Austen's Pride and Prejudice: The Study Guide Edition (2015)
Mary Shelley's Frankenstein: The Study Guide Edition (2015)

Contents

Part 1: Introduction

This study guide takes a different approach from most other similar books. It does not seek to tell you about the story and characters in a boring, useless fashion, but attempts to show how it is the author's techniques and interests that inform every single facet of this classic novel. Most study guides simply tell you *what* is going on, and tack on bits at the end which tell you *how* the writer created suspense and drama at certain points in the book, informing you a little about *why* the writer might have done this.

This study guide starts with the *how* and the *why*, showing you right from the start *how* and *why* the writer shaped the key elements of the book.

Definition:

The context of a book is both the *world* the book creates in the reader's mind (contexts of reading), and the *world* it came out from (contexts of writing).

How to use this Study Guide

This guide is deliberately interactive; it is full of questions, tasks and links to other sources of information. You will learn about *Wuthering Heights* much more effectively if you have a go at the questions and tasks set, rather than just copying out notes.

Contexts

Understanding Contexts

In order to fully appreciate a text, you need to appreciate the contexts in which it was written – known as its contexts of writing – and the contexts in which you read the book, or the contexts of reading.

This is potentially a huge area to explore because 'contexts' essentially means the 'worlds' from which the book has arisen. For the best books, these are many and various. The most obvious starting point is the writer's own life: it is worth thinking about how and why the events in a writer's life might have influenced his or her fiction. However, you do have to be careful not to assume too much. For example, many critics have sort parallels between Emily Brontë's life and the world of the book, claiming that the alcoholic, abusive Hindley is based upon Brontë's drunken brother but you must remember that Hindley is a character in her own right in the novel – a vital cog in the narrative wheel, a literary construct and not a real person!

As a result, it is particularly fruitful to explore other contexts of writing. We can look at the broader world from which Emily Brontë arose (early Victorian society and its set of values), and consider carefully how, in her writing, she both adopted and rejected the morals of her time. Other contexts might be the influence of the literary world that Brontë inhabited (what other authors were writing at the time), how religion shaped her views, and so on.

Just as important as the contexts of *writing* are the contexts of *reading*: how we read the novel today. Many of us will have seen one or more of the many film versions of the book, and/or been influenced by what we have already heard about the Brontës Your own personal context is very important too. This is famously a 'girl's' book, with the stereotype being that teenage girls fall in love with Heathcliff's passionate, brutal character. However, having taught it for a number of years, I have found that boys respond well to it too. In order for you to fully consider the contexts of reading rather than my telling you what to think, I have posed open-ended questions that seem to me to be important when considering this issue.

Questions

What do we mean by context? Why do you need to understand the idea of context in order to write well about *Wuthering Heights*?

Useful links

This handout produced by the University of Carolina is very clear and useful, full of good suggestions about how to write well about fiction, including useful comments about context:
http://writingcenter.unc.edu/handouts/literature-fiction/
This paper is aimed at teachers, but is full of excellent points for students too:
http://education.cambridge.org/media/577064/world_and_ti me__teaching_literature_in_context___cambridge_education ___cambridge_university_press_samples.pdf

Contexts of Writing: Emily Brontë's Life

Emily Brontë was the most intense and spiritual of the talented Brontë sisters. Born in 1818, she was the younger sister of Charlotte Brontë, who famously wrote *Jane Eyre*, but older than Anne, who wrote a devastating novel about alcoholism called *The Tenant At Wildfell Hall*. Although born in Thornton, near Bradford in Yorkshire, she and her sisters are most associated with Haworth, where Emily father's was a religious man, a curate. Haworth is now a place of pilgrimage for the legions of fans of the Brontës but it still retains the essential qualities it had when the Brontës were alive: its isolated, bleak setting on the moors, its Gothic qualities.

In 1821, their mother died, shortly after the move to Haworth; this appears to have led to the sisters becoming very close. It appears that Charlotte became the most dominant figure, although there is some evidence that Emily played a vital role in soothing her troubled sister's nerves, despite her poor health.

In 1824, Emily joined her sisters Maria, Elizabeth and Charlotte at Cowan Bridge school for daughters of the clergy. This school was memorably portrayed as Lowood school in Charlotte Brontë's *Jane Eyre*; the picture that Charlotte paints is not a pretty one. The school was a cesspit for disease and rigid, terrifying discipline. Some biographers have speculated that Charlotte based her saintly character of Helen Burns on Emily: there is a strong likelihood that Emily developed her strong religious beliefs at the school. A running theme for Emily and in Wuthering Heights is the superiority of the after-life to life on earth: it's a view that Charlotte rejected in her work, but Emily strongly emphasises the amazing spiritual qualities of heaven. These are similar arguments to those of Helen Burns in *Jane Eyre*.

In 1825, suffering from the appallingly unsanitary conditions at the school, Maria was sent home ill from school and died in early May; Emily was removed the following day. Her sister Elizabeth died in June of that year. These terrible tragedies undoubtedly brought the surviving children more strongly together. The sisters and their brother, Branwell, sort refuge from the vicissitudes of world by creating imaginary lands. After being initially inspired by Branwell's receipt of toy soldiers, the children went onto create huge fantasies; constructing stories, poems, plays and fables from their invented characters.

In 1831, Charlotte and Emily began to create their own stories known as the Gondal saga. They drew pictures of it, scribbled innumerable stories about it, and pretended to be characters in it. Not much of Emily's work from this period survives but there are tiny scraps about Gondal in the **Brontë Parsonage Museum at Haworth** and the **British Library**.

As a teenager, in 1835, Emily attended Roe Head school, but suffered from terrible homesickness and returned to Haworth after only three months, with her health severely deteriorating. Anne replaced Emily at Roe

Head. The following year, Emily wrote her first known poem, 'Will the day be bright or cloudy?'. In 1837, she wrote a further nineteen poems. Now keen to pay her own way in a household in financial trouble, Emily took a position as a junior teacher at Law Hill girls' school, but once again her poor health precipitated a collapse and she returned home in the spring of 1839, where she wrote another twenty-one poems. The following years were taken up with poetry writing; over half of her surviving poems were written at this time. In 1841, Emily wrote in her diary: "A scheme is at present in agitation for setting us up in a school of our own." The next year, Emily accompanied Charlotte to Brussels to M. Heger's school for girls. Much has been made by biographers of the influence that the trip to Brussels had on Charlotte because it's so well documented, however, little is known about the influence it had upon Emily. But we must assume that it did have a huge influence for such a sheltered girl like Emily; what's difficult to work out is how it influenced her. Much in the same way that Heathcliff returns to Wuthering Heights mysteriously and almost inexplicably changed, we will never know what happened to Emily in Brussels.

Unfortunately, later on that year, more tragedy dogged them because their Aunt Elizabeth Branwell died, which caused both Charlotte and Emily to leave Brussels. Emily's time in Brussels was clearly very formative: it was here that she was exposed to a wide variety of Romantic literature and art, much of which inspired the texture, characters and prose of Wuthering Heights. However, possibly troubled by her sister's romantic attachment to the married M. Heger, Emily refused to return to Brussels the following year. In December, a degree of financial relief occurred, when the sisters learnt that they had inherited approximately £300 from Aunt Branwell.

In 1844, Emily copies poetry in two book entitled 'Gondal Poems' and 'EJB'. The following year, she and Anne took a three day trip to York – a very rare event for such a hermetically sealed person as Emily, who was the ultimate 'homebody'. In the autumn of that year, Charlotte discovered Emily's poetry and persuaded her to seek publication of it. In 1846, the poems were published pseudonymously as *Poems by Currer, Ellis, and Acton Bell* at the sisters' expense. Later on, in July, Charlotte wrote to the London publisher, Henry Colburn, offering 'three tales, each occupying a volume and capable of being published together or separately; these stories were Charlotte's *The Professor*, Emily's *Wuthering Heights*, and Anne's *Agnes Grey*. In 1847, Charlotte publishes Jane Eyre after her first novel, *The Professor*, was rejected by numerous publishers. In December of that year, *Wuthering Heights* was published in a single edition with *Agnes Grey*. In 1848, after terrorising his sisters and father with his alcoholic rages, Branwell died in an alcoholic stupor. Now dying of consumption after years of ill-health, Emily died in December of that year.

Although not much is known about the circumstances surrounding the writing of *Wuthering Heights*, we can speculate this is how it was written. Emily and Charlotte evolved a clear method of working when they were both at home: they would discuss their work and plans together in the same drawing room until 11am, at which time they would settle down to write. A diary note, penned by Anne and Emily's diary, from the late 1830s, gives us a good clue:

> Monday evening June 26th 1837 A bit past 4 o'clock Charlotte working in Aunt's room, Branwell reading Eugene Aram to her—Anne and I writing in the drawing-room—Anne a poem beginning "Fair was the evening and brightly the sun"—I Augusta Almeda's life 1st V. 1-4th page from the last—fine rather coolish thin grey cloudy but sunny day Aunt working in the little room the old nursery Papa gone out Tabby in the kitchen—the Emperors and Empresses of Gondal and Gaaldine preparing to depart from Gaaldine to Gondal to prepare for the coronation which will be on the 12th July Queen Victoria ascended the throne this month. Northangerland in Monkey's Isle—Zamora at Eversham. All tight and right in which condition it is hoped we shall all be this day 4 years at which time Charlotte will be 25 and 2 months Branwell just 24 it being his birthday—myself 22 and 10 months and a piece Anne 21 and nearly a half I wonder where we shall be and how we shall be and what kind of a day it will be then— let us hope for the best

It is fascinating to see here how little the outside world impinges upon the Brontës: a monumental event like the coronation of Queen Victoria is a mere footnote compared with the imaginative world of Gondal. The house appears to be a hive of industry, with the sisters all working extremely hard at their writing. There is no doubt that the characters from Wuthering Heights had their origins in Gondal: their extravagant emotions, their wild fits of rage, the melodramatic events are clearly things that happened in Gondal. However, certain things like Hindley's alcoholism were clearly based on Emily's brother Branwell, who, after appearing to be the golden-eyed boy of the family, descended into a trough of depression and drink.

Much has been speculated about Emily's life, but in truth very little is known about her; only the scraps we have from her diaries; nearly everything we know has been filtered through Charlotte, who outlived her. Charlotte's novel *Shirley* with its central character of the same name being a headstrong, independent heroine is thought to be a portrait of Emily by some critics. Early biographers sort to depict her as a religious saint, an almost idiot savant, someone who was in contact with the spiritual world. However, more recent biographers have pieced together a more convincing picture of a woman who was an avid reader absorbing a great deal of literature. Above all, Emily was a master craftsman: her poetry is beautifully constructed, and Wuthering Heights, as we will see, is a marvellously architectural novel, and incredibly carefully structured.

Questions

Find out more about where the Brontës lived and the place Wuthering Heights is supposedly based upon Why do you think the book might be called *Wuthering Heights*?

What events, people and ideas in Brontë's life and the wider society may have influenced the writing of *Wuthering Heights*? Why is it important to consider her gender, her family, her friends and her reading when studying the book?

Useful links

The British Library has some excellent resources on Emily Brontë:
http://www.bl.uk/people/emily-bronte
The Victorian Web has a good reliable biography:
http://www.victorianweb.org/authors/bronte/ebronte/bio.ht ml
There are useful links on this webpage too as well as links to other topics connected with the novel:
http://academic.brooklyn.cuny.edu/english/melani/novel_19c /wuthering/

Selected Reading on Emily Brontë's Life

Juliet Barker: *The Brontës* (Phoenix; 1994)
A landmark book on the family, brilliantly researched.
Robert Barnard: *Emily Brontë* (British Library Writer's lives; 2000)
A short but persuasive biography which shows how *Wuthering Heights* was very influenced by the events in Brontë 's life.

Contexts of Reading

The Brontës still hold a huge grip on the reading public's imagination. If anything, *Wuthering Heights* has come, in recent years, to eclipse *Jane Eyre* as the most popular Brontë novel. At the time of its publication, the novel shocked many of its readers, particularly with the way it seemed irreligious: Heathcliff and Cathy are both characters who attain heaven by being ungodly. They are, in no senses, virtuous characters: Heathcliff is a violent, rapacious, revengeful, resentful lover, and Cathy is presented as spiteful, petty and mean. Yet, it is clear at the end of the novel that they have attained their own heaven: they are re-united in death.

Heathcliff shares much in common with Charlotte's Mr Rochester: both are deceitful, passionate, tempestuous men. However, Heathcliff is a more extreme characterisation. His villainy goes much further than anything Rochester is guilty of. Yet, he is perhaps the most popular of all Romantic heroes. Why is this? In our modern times, we have much more sympathy for the under-dog than the Victorians did. The racism and abuse that Heathcliff suffers at the hands of his chief tormentor, Hindley, is something that has become even more relevant now: we as a society look upon this sort of prejudice as one of the most divisive and cruel in a way that the Victorians never did. In this sense, the novel is very modern.

The melodrama of the major episodes has a realistic quality which makes the novel have much in common with the modern-day soap opera such as *Eastenders* or *Coronation Street*. Brontë, in her scenes between the embittered Hindley and Heathcliff, the drunk Hindley and his small son Hareton, in her depictions of the strife between Linton and Cathy (both generations!), has an eye for the domestic drama which has been much imitated. The novel shows how tiny details such jealousy over a dress can trigger huge rows. Obviously, the great passionate love scenes seem more dated: modern writers and film makers are not so comfortable with such outpourings of love. However, the modern reading public hasn't lost their appetite for them and seem to seek them in novels like *Wuthering Heights*, where, unlike the modern novel, they are permitted to happen with ironic commentary. In this sense, *Wuthering Heights* gives modern readers what they can never find in contemporary fiction: truly passionate depictions of love.

Questions

It is worth doing some work on contexts before starting the actual book. I would suggest you write a *Wuthering Heights* **learning journal** that records all your thoughts and feelings about the book. Records the truth! After reading the book once, we will then look at academic responses but on the first reading we will really focus upon your thoughts about it.

There are two major questions to consider when thinking about contexts: where is the book coming from and where am I coming from?

The first question is best answered while reading the book; what sorts of values and ideas are enshrined in this book? What is its historical context? What is its literary context? What is its philosophical context? How does the book relate to the life of the author?

It is worth you trying to analyse where you are coming from. Everyone holds a set of assumptions and ideas that profoundly affects how he or she sees the world. Try and answer these questions:

What are your attitudes towards male and female relationships?

What are your attitudes towards love? Do you think love affairs can ever end well? Can love be eternal?

What are your attitudes towards families? Do you think they are a force for good or not? Think about your own family; why do terrible arguments/rows happen in families, and yet huge love as well? Why are human beings still very attached to concepts of the family, despite all the changes that have happened in society over the last few centuries?

What is your attitude towards nature and remote places? Do you like or loathe them?

Useful links

This Wikipedia page contains information about the various adaptations of the novel:

**https://en.wikipedia.org/wiki/Adaptations_of_Wuthering_He
ights**

You can find more about adaptations here:

http://www.wuthering-heights.co.uk/watch.php

The IMBD website also contains a list of the various mainstream films
made of the novel:

http://www.imdb.com/list/ls051654736/

There are some musings about the modern day impact of *Wuthering
Heights* here:

http://www.wuthering-heights.co.uk/musings.php

This Guardian article about the popularity of the novel is useful:

**http://www.theguardian.com/uk/2007/aug/10/books.booksne
ws**

Now onto the text

What are the vital ingredients of a story? Why is that we are able to
believe that a "whole load of words" contain a new world?

Now jot down your expectations about *Wuthering Heights*. What kind of
book do you expect it to be?

Write out what you think the story will be. Write out how you think it will
be structured. What will be the main events of the story? Who will be the
main characters?

While reading the novel, look back over the notes you have made for this
section and constantly ask yourself; how does my context affect the way I
read the novel and feel/think about the characters/situations/themes? I
have already suggested that you write a learning journal as you read it
through, jotting down these thoughts as you go along. Then once you have
finished reading, think about the novel's overall effects and how it speaks
to you personally.

Why do you think *Wuthering Heights* is such a popular novel today?
Why have so many films/plays etc. been made of it?

Structure and Theme

Many critics have noted that *Wuthering Heights* is one of the most beautifully structured novels ever written: there is a beautiful symmetry about the novel which is endlessly gratifying and intriguing. Ultimately, the novel explores the theme of how the past influences the present, how the crimes of yesteryear impact upon the present day: the pleasure of re-reading the novel is the way in which the reader can see this in so many different ways. Every time I re-read the novel, I see some link between the past and the present which I hadn't seen before. The novel can be confusing because it is not a 'linear' narrative: the action does not happen chronologically. Instead, Brontë constantly weaves between the present day and the past. In order to create this sense of the past affecting the present, Brontë effectively writes not one but two narratives; that's why the novel must be analysed as two separate narratives which inform each other.

We could break down the novel into the following structure:

Opening

1801. Lockwood sees Cathy's ghost while stranded at *Wuthering Heights*. Heathcliff begs for Cathy to come back to him.

Lockwood returns to Thrushcross Grange, where he is staying, where the servant Nelly Dean begins to tell him the story of *Wuthering Heights*.

Complications

Nelly's account tells us about thirty years before Heathcliff and Cathy's childhood, Heathcliff's mysterious origins, Earnshaw's profound, doting love for him. The closeness between Cathy and Heathcliff. Hindley's jealousy.

Earnshaw dies in 1774, and Hindley returns to Wuthering Heights with his silly wife, Frances, who dies giving birth to Hareton. Hindley takes to drink and his abuse of Heathcliff becomes appalling.

Crisis

Cathy meets Edgar Linton while sniggering at Edgar and his sister Isabella arguing. She tells Nelly that it would be degrading to marry Heathcliff who is beneath her socially. Heathcliff disappears, Cathy becomes dreadfully ill, and is nursed back to health by Edgar. Later she marries him.

Climax

Heathcliff returns much to the happiness of Cathy: he takes over Wuthering Heights after Hindley dies hugely in debt to the now wealthy Heathcliff. Isabella becomes besotted by Heathcliff: they elope. Cathy and Heathcliff row over Isabella.

Resolution

Before Cathy dies giving birth to her daughter Catherine, Heathcliff and she are reconciled.

Opening

Twelve years later, the dying Isabella who has fled from the brutal Heathcliff, asks Edgar to care for her son, Linton. Heathcliff won't have this, and takes charge of Linton, who is his son, treating him with secret contempt.

The young Cathy now takes an interest in her son and is resentful of her father's reluctance for her to go to Wuthering Heights.

Complications

Heathcliff kidnaps Cathy and forces her to marry Linton Heathcliff, his son. Soon after Edgar Linton dies.

Linton Heathcliff dies; Heathcliff inherits all his son's property, including Thrushcross Grange. His revenge is complete.

Cathy is a widow and prisoner at Wuthering Heights.

We realise this is the time when Lockwood visited them.

Crisis

Lockwood returns to the area a year later and learns that Heathcliff is dead. Nelly tells him the remaining narrative.

Cathy and Hareton begin to become close: she teaches him how to read and ceases to mock him.

With the backing and protection of Hareton, Cathy begins to stand up to Heathcliff. Seeing their love for one another and perhaps prompted by Lockwood's encounter with the ghost, Heathcliff seems to suffer a mental breakdown and believes he can see Cathy's ghost.

Climax

Believing he will see Cathy after he dies, Heathcliff gives up on attaining revenge and effectively commits suicide by refusing food and drink, and lying in bed with the windows open. His hand is outstretched as if holding Cathy's hand.

Resolution

Heathcliff is buried next to Catherine. Several villagers swear that they have seen their ghosts together on the moors.

Lockwood visits their graves observing how restful they seem.

Useful links to help you get to know the novel better

There are a number of quizzes on the novel which are useful to get to know the basics of the novel. They are multiple choice:

http://www.gradesaver.com/wuthering-heights/study-guide/quiz1

http://www.sparknotes.com/lit/wuthering/quiz.html

http://www.cliffsnotes.com/literature/w/wuthering-heights/study-help/quiz

http://www.shmoop.com/wuthering-heights/quizzes.html

http://blog.oup.com/2015/03/wuthering-heights-quiz/
The above websites also have some clear summaries of the novel, which are helpful to look at if you are struggling to follow the story.

Questions/tasks

Once you have read the book, ask yourself this question: to what extent is the novel a successful story? What are its exciting moments and why? Are there moments when the story feels less successful? Give reasons for your answers.

Compare one or two filmed versions with the novel; what events/characters/ideas do the film-makers use and what do they leave out, and why?

The Influence of Genre

The Revenger's Tragedy

Many critics have noted how the novel is very influenced by the genre of the Gothic. Heathcliff, at times, is like a Gothic villain: this is particularly the case when he locks Cathy up and keeps her a prisoner in the haunted Wuthering Heights. The Gothic was a genre that emerged in the eighteenth century. Gothic novels were usually about a scheming villain who lures a pretty girl to his haunted castle, hoping to have his wicked way with her. The narratives were coloured with plenty of descriptions of ghosts, secret passageways and mysterious, spooky goings-on. Brontë's novel has all of these elements, but, as we have seen, its psychological complexities make it far more than an ordinary Gothic novel.

This is most obviously illustrated in Brontë's characterisation of Heathcliff. While he has elements of being a villain, he is also a Romantic anti-hero: he speaks poetically about his love for Cathy and the moors and acts passionately to fight for justice at key moments in the novel.

But for all his connections to the Gothic novel and Romantic heroes like Lord Byron, Heathcliff is most intent upon revenge for much of the novel: this is what motivates many of his actions. In this sense, the novel shares more in common with Shakespeare's tragedies and Jacobean plays in general than novels of the period: like Bosola in Webster's *The Duchess Of Malfi*, Heathcliff is a villain who seeks justice and revenge. His return to Wuthering Heights is motivated not only by his love for Cathy but by revenge: he manages to gain his revenge upon the abusive Hindley by putting him in his debt, and he gains his revenge upon Edgar by winning back the love of his wife, Cathy. After Cathy dies, he revenges himself further upon Edgar Linton by imprisoning his daughter and forcing him to marry his limp son. His revenge is complete when Linton and his son die, and he now owns all the property that he was so excluded from as a child. But, as with all tragedies, revenge is not enough: there is an emptiness to it. Believing he can re-unite himself with Cathy, he precipitates his own death.

Questions for Genre

How was Brontë influenced by other writers and genres in the writing of *Wuthering Heights*? Where did she get her ideas for her characters from? Think for about the influences of the imaginary worlds the sisters devised.

Useful links

The best place to start for learning about the Gothic in more depth is the British Library website:

http://www.bl.uk/romantics-and-victorians/videos/the-gothic

The British Library also has a good article on the ways in which the novel blends realism and fantasy here:

http://www.bl.uk/romantics-and-victorians/articles/melding-of-fantasy-and-realism-in-wuthering-heights

The BBC have a great many resources on the Gothic with links to radio programmes on important texts:

http://www.bbc.co.uk/timelines/zyp72hv
http://www.bbc.co.uk/programmes/po2832f5

The Shmoop website lists the different genres at work in the novel:

http://www.shmoop.com/wuthering-heights/genre.html

There is a good explanation of the Gothic here:

http://academic.brooklyn.cuny.edu/english/melani/novel_19c/wuthering/gothic.html

The same website has an explanation of the Romantic elements of the novel here:

http://academic.brooklyn.cuny.edu/english/melani/novel_19c/wuthering/romantic.html

This 1989 academic essay by Lyn Pickett is exhaustive in its exploration of the different genre influences in the novel:

http://homepage.ntlworld.com/chris.thorns/resources/Wuthering%20Heights/Gender_and_Genre.pdf

Critical Perspectives

Is *Wuthering Heights* really a love story?

Many readers would think it a sacrilege to even ask this question. True devotees of the book might wail: 'Of course, it's a love story; it's all about the undying, passionate love between Cathy and Heathcliff!' Indeed, there is much evidence for this point. Heathcliff and Cathy appear to have a love which transcends everything: social class, the vagaries of fate, illness, husbands and wives, errant parents, nature -- even death itself. The two of them appear to share bond of understanding which while it is expressed in words in the novel, clearly falls outside words. Cathy's declaration 'I am Heathcliff' is, on the surface, a perfect articulation of her love for Heathcliff, but also suggests that her love for him has a profoundly mystical quality: somehow his personality has merged with hers and they are the same person.

In Chapter IX, Cathy claims that her miseries are Heathcliff's miseries and that her great thought in living is Heathcliff. In other words, Cathy feels her life is totally subsumed by Heathcliff. This is an interesting train of thought to follow in the novel. If she is indeed Heathcliff, and Heathcliff is her, then her death in the novel means that Heathcliff becomes Cathy's sole embodiment on earth; his actions which torment her daughter and her husband are indeed her actions. He is not only taking revenge upon them for his own gratification, but also because he is a vehicle for Cathy's own vicious desire for revenge against the child who killed her (she effectively dies giving birth) and the husband who crushed her spirit, and denied her Heathcliff, her true love.

Cathy claims that Nelly's anxiety that her marriage to Edgar Linton will mean Heathcliff will feel rejected is utter rubbish. She says: "This is for the sake of one who comprehends in his person my feeling to Edgar and myself". But she is wrong here: Heathcliff is so profoundly disappointed and hurt that he disappears for three years. In other words, she reveals that she is not Heathcliff at all; far from it, she hardly understands him at all. His bitterness at her marriage to Linton is scarcely comprehended by her. Some critics have noted that what Cathy does is to 'project' her ideal love onto Heathcliff, while failing to see the real person.

Indeed, many people misunderstand Heathcliff in the novel: one of the major things about him is that he is such a mysterious character. We don't know where he has come from, we don't know what he does when disappears for three years, and we never fully appreciate his complex relationships with those around him. At times, he is the Gothic villain, imprisoning the younger Cathy with his nefarious plot to get her to marry his son, at other times, he is a surrogate father who inspires a God-like devotion in the abused Hareton, while at others, he is the passionate, misunderstood lover; sometimes, he is the Romantic poet, understanding and absorbing the mysteries of nature. Finally, he is the suicidal Christian lover, who believes he will attain heaven and Cathy by killing himself, despite the teachings of the church that suicide takes you straight to hell.

What is more, bar a few brief lines about their joyous romps across the moors, which are delivered after the event, we rarely seen, in detail, Cathy and Heathcliff happy together. Furthermore, they seem to be closest when they are most tortured by each other: the powerful scene between Cathy and Heathcliff just before she dies is characterised by her tormenting Heathcliff about her death. Examined closely, they are almost the polar opposites of the perfect lovers: they are forever at odds with one another. However, what they do is yearn for a perfect love, which they claim they have found in each other. Heathcliff and Cathy project their desire for a perfect love onto each other.

In such a way, we could say that the novel is not a love story, but almost a psychoanalytical parable about people's desires for a perfect lover. Indeed, many critics have noted the novel's psychological qualities. It lends itself to various psycho-analytical readings. Freudian critics, who believe that novels can be interpreted according to the principles of psycho-analysis laid down by Freud, might see the novel as having Oedipal qualities. Heathcliff, like Oedipus, in the Greek play, effectively kills the father figure of Hindley and yearns to gain the love of Cathy, who was the motherly figure during his childhood.

Marxist critics have perceived that the novel can only be understood when the issue of social class is taken into account. Heathcliff's love for Cathy is the love of the dispossessed underclass for the property that is rightfully theirs, but denied to them. Heathcliff is exploited by the upper class Hindley and rebels against him as a result. His taking over of Wuthering Heights and Thrushcross Grange is a form of proletarian revolution. The one thing he can't have is Cathy because she is now dead: his only way to claim her is to die. Thus, his suicide is a revolutionary act as well: he is snatching Cathy from her husband by being buried with her.

These modern qualities about the novel -- Heathcliff's revolutionary spirit, the obsessive, co-dependent love between Cathy and Heathcliff, the Oedipal qualities in the novel – have all meant that the novel has continued to fascinate critics and the public alike: it is the way the novel ultimately eludes any one interpretation which makes so great.

Selected Reading and weblinks on *Wuthering Heights*

There are a collection what various critics have said about the novel here:
http://www.wuthering-heights.co.uk/reviews.php
There is an interesting comment piece from Martin Kettle explaining why

he thinks it is not a love story here:

**http://www.theguardian.com/commentisfree/2007/aug/11/co
mment.bookscomment**

There is a clear explanation of feminist interpretations of the novel here:

**http://academic.brooklyn.cuny.edu/english/melani/novel_19c
/wuthering/gothic.html**

Other critical views are explained here:

**http://academic.brooklyn.cuny.edu/english/melani/novel_19c
/wuthering/critics.html**

There is a clear but brief guide to different critical approaches here:

http://crossref-it.info/textguide/wuthering-heights/35/2535

The Teacher's Guide to the Signet Classic Edition of Wuthering Heights is useful not only for teachers but also students:

**https://www.ucm.es/data/cont/docs/119-2014-04-09-
GuideTo%20Wuthering%20Heights.pdf**

Barbara and Gareth Lloyd Evans: *Everyman's Companion to the Brontës* (J.M. Dent and Sons: 1982) A gushing, old fashioned, rather hysterical account of *Wuthering Heights* is included here, but it is very readable and provides plenty to think about – even if you don't agree with it.

Felicia Gordon: *A Preface to the Brontës* (Longman; 1989)

Part of the Longman Preface series. Of all the A-level guides, this remains the best short introduction to the Brontës that there is: Gordon's concise grasp of the historical and literary context makes this my favourite Preface book of this superb series.

Heather Glen (editor): The Cambridge Companion To The *Brontës* (CUP: 2002) All the latest critical thinking about the novel is here in a very readable form.

Questions

What differing views do literary critics have of the novel? Which critics do you most agree with and why? Which ones do you agree with the least and why?

Part 2: Extracts & questions

How to read and study the novel

What follows are selected extracts from *Wuthering Heights* interspersed with commentaries and questions on the text. I have deliberately provided a variety of different question types at the ends of chapters; I have started with "simple" comprehension questions and then moved onto more analytical and creative questions, which not only require you to understand the plot but also arrive at your own personal responses, using evidence from the text to back up your points. I have provided **brief answers** to the comprehension questions and some pointers for the other questions in the section **'Answers to the questions'**. The GCSE/A Level questions that follow the comprehension ones are more difficult and don't usually have "right and wrong" answers. The GCSE style questions are the sorts of questions you might typically get in a GCSE exam; the same is true for the A Level questions, which usually invite students to show they have read more and are able to compare and contrast texts in depth. Please interpret the categories of GCSE/A Level in a relaxed fashion: have a go at the exercises which will help you rather than rigidly sticking to the exercises that are "your level". The categories are only rough guidelines. I sometimes ask you to devise a visual organiser to represent ideas/characters/plot-lines in the novel; this means doing a spider-diagram/chart/flow diagram etc. depending upon what you feel is most relevant. To find out more (sometimes known as graphic organisers) look here:

https://www.teachingenglish.org.uk/article/graphic-organisers

Remember if you are uncertain about the plot, you can also refer to the websites listed in the section **'Useful links to help you get to know the story better'**. These websites are good at helping you understand the plot but they won't help you get the higher marks because you really need to think for yourself if you are going to get the top grades.

You could, while reading the book, put all your answers, notes, creative responses together into a *Wuthering Heights* file or **learning journal**. You could be creative with this file: draw scenes of the important incidents; include spider-diagrams/visual organisers of significant characters and situations; storyboards of the key scenes; copies of articles/literary criticism which you have annotated; creative pieces etc.

Helpful vocabulary to learn before you start reading

You should keep **a vocabulary list**, writing down the difficult words and learning their meanings/spellings, and possibly using the vocabulary in your own writing. The dialect in *Wuthering Heights* can be off-putting at first but the websites listed below will give you good translations of it. Don't be put off by the language; embrace it, love it! You will become much better educated when you learn the vocabulary. This is why reading pre-20th century writing is so useful: it makes you more intelligent because you widen your vocabulary and ability to understand difficult passages.

There are some words, I would strongly advise you looking up the meanings of and learning their spellings/meanings before reading; the websites listed below are helpful in this regard.

Weblinks to help you learn difficult vocabulary

Vocabulary.com has an exhaustive list of the difficult vocabulary with it explained in context:
http://www.vocabulary.com/lists/25183#view=notes
This Word document contains a very useful grid for charting the difficult vocabulary in context:
http://www.ahsd.org/english/conigliaro/Wuthering%20Heights %20Reading%20Analysis%20Vocabulary%20and%20Study%20 Materials%20Packet%202009.doc
Spark Notes has a good section where it explains the important quotes:
http://www.sparknotes.com/lit/wuthering/quotes.html
There is a very useful explanation of Joseph's speech here:
http://www.wuthering-heights.co.uk/josephs-speech.php
And a good glossary of his language here:
http://www.wuthering-heights.co.uk/glossary.php
There is an excellent explanation of the dialect by Stevie Davies here:
http://www.swanseareview.com/2012/steviedavies.html

CHAPTER 1

Extract

1801.—I have just returned from a visit to my landlord—the solitary neighbour that I shall be troubled with. This is certainly a beautiful country! In all England, I do not believe that I could have fixed on a situation so completely removed from the stir of society. A perfect misanthropist's heaven: and Mr. Heathcliff and I are such a suitable pair to divide the desolation between us. A capital fellow! He little imagined how my heart warmed towards him when I beheld his black eyes withdraw so suspiciously under their brows, as I rode up, and when his fingers sheltered themselves, with a jealous resolution, still further in his waistcoat, as I announced my name.

'Mr. Heathcliff?' I said.

A nod was the answer.

Analysis: The novel opens with Lockwood, a gentleman from London, talking about the reasons why he has escaped to the remote Yorkshire moors. He is a self-proclaimed 'misanthropist' – a person who wishes to shun society. However, we quickly realise that Lockwood is not a reliable commentator because he actually does his best to seek out company in this remote world, taking a visit to Wuthering Heights, a remote farmhouse on the windy moors. Brontë establishes both setting and character very quickly: the contrast between the falsely jolly Lockwood and the sullen Heathcliff. She is a master at dramatisation: showing not telling. Notice how so much is revealed about Heathcliff in the 'nod' – he utters few words, but it is obvious that his body speaks to people.

Discussion point: How successful is the opening to the novel in enticing the reader to read more? What mysteries and problems are established?

Extract

Wuthering Heights is the name of Mr. Heathcliff's dwelling. 'Wuthering' being a significant provincial adjective, descriptive of the atmospheric tumult to which its station is exposed in stormy weather. Pure, bracing ventilation they must have up there at all times, indeed: one may guess the power of the north wind blowing over the edge, by the excessive slant of a few stunted firs at the end of the house; and by a range of gaunt thorns all stretching their limbs one way, as if craving alms of the sun. Happily, the architect had foresight to build it strong: the narrow windows are deeply set in the wall, and the corners defended with large jutting stones.

Analysis: Fascinatingly, Brontë chose 'wuthering' to be adjective in her title: a local dialect word meaning 'windy'. How different the novel would be if it were called 'Windy Heights'!

Discussion point: Why did Brontë name the novel 'Wuthering Heights'? What is the effect of this powerful adjective?

Extract

'You'd better let the dog alone,' growled Mr. Heathcliff in unison, checking fiercer demonstrations with a punch of his foot. 'She's not accustomed to be spoiled—not kept for a pet.' Then, striding to a side door, he shouted again, 'Joseph!'

Joseph mumbled indistinctly in the depths of the cellar, but gave no intimation of ascending; so his master dived down to him, leaving me vis-à-vis the ruffianly bitch and a pair of grim shaggy sheep-dogs, who shared with her a jealous guardianship over all my movements. Not anxious to come in contact with their fangs, I sat still; but, imagining they would scarcely understand tacit insults, I unfortunately indulged in winking and making faces at the trio, and some turn of my physiognomy so irritated madam, that she suddenly broke into a fury and leapt on my knees. I flung her back, and hastened to interpose the table between us. This proceeding aroused the whole hive: half-a-dozen four-footed fiends, of various sizes and ages, issued from hidden dens to the common centre. I felt my heels and coat-laps peculiar subjects of assault; and parrying off the larger combatants as effectually as I could with the poker, I was constrained to demand, aloud, assistance from some of the household in re-establishing peace.

> Brontë's descriptions of farm life: the 'frenzied, huge, liver-coloured bitch pointer', the 'swarm of squealing puppies', the 'dark-skinned gypsy' qualities of Heathcliff, and the 'mumbling' Joseph are so vivid that we have a sense of an entire life being lived at the farm. She presents a farm which is clearly a working one – there is a great sense of rush and tumble – but it is clearly a very unhappy one. The bitches' attack on Lockwood suggests a very aggressive atmosphere in the place: the dogs mirror their masters' moods.

Discussion point:_Why is the attack on Lockwood so shocking? Have you ever been attacked by a dog? What do dogs tell us about their masters?

Questions

What house is Mr Lockwood renting and why?
What does 'wuthering' mean?
What is the penetralium?

How friendly are Heathcliff and Joseph?

What condition is the property in at Wuthering Heights?

What interests Lockwood which is over the door and why?

Why is Lockwood interested by Heathcliff?

What happens when he is left in a room?

Devise a **visual organizer** of the key events/literary techniques in the chapter.

GCSE style question: how effective is this opening to the novel? What are its strengths and weaknesses?

A Level style question: compare and contrast this opening with other relevant openings of relevant literature.

Creative response: write a short story or poem called 'The Visit' in which you describe a strange place you have visited.

Please find brief answers in section: **answers to questions**.

CHAPTER 2

Extract

'Mrs. Heathcliff is my daughter-in-law,' said Heathcliff, corroborating my surmise. He turned, as he spoke, a peculiar look in her direction: a look of hatred; unless he has a most perverse set of facial muscles that will not, like those of other people, interpret the language of his soul.

'Ah, certainly—I see now: you are the favoured possessor of the beneficent fairy,' I remarked, turning to my neighbour.

This was worse than before: the youth grew crimson, and clenched his fist, with every appearance of a meditated assault. But he seemed to recollect himself presently, and smothered the storm in a brutal curse, muttered on my behalf: which, however, I took care not to notice.

'Unhappy in your conjectures, sir,' observed my host; 'we neither of us have the privilege of owning your good fairy; her mate is dead. I said she was my daughter-in-law: therefore, she must have married my son.'

'And this young man is—'

'Not my son, assuredly.'

Heathcliff smiled again, as if it were rather too bold a jest to attribute the paternity of that bear to him.

'My name is Hareton Earnshaw,' growled the other; 'and I'd counsel you to respect it!'

Analysis: After the shock and drama of the dog attack, we now have the high comedy of Lockwood failing to understand or appreciate the complexities of the relationships in the house. He gets everything wrong in much the same way that the reader does on first reading – and possibly many other readings after that! Heathcliff's response is darkly ironic, deliberately comic. The scene is also important in that it establishes a rapport between Lockwood and the reader: he is as confused as we are. His discovery of the truth about

Wuthering Heights is our discovery: he is our pathway into the novel. Even though we may feel dubious about him as a person, he is undoubtedly the person we most associate with at this point in the novel.

Discussion point: What evidence is there that Heathcliff is mocking Lockwood here? Why did Brontë include this scene in the novel?

Questions

Who does Lockwood mistake the young, unfriendly girl for?
What does he later assume about the girl?
What does he think of the young man?
What does he later learn about the girl and man?
What happens to the weather after supper?
What does Lockwood do when no one will help him home?
Why does he not get home?
Who is the housekeeper and how does she help Lockwood?
Why do we learn that Lockwood is an unreliable narrator in this chapter?
Why are all the doors and gates barred and chained?
What does 'whisht' mean?
GCSE style question: How does Brontë create a sense of menace and confusion in this chapter?
A Level style question: compare and contrast the ways in which other relevant literature creates a sense of menace.
Creative response: write a poem/story called 'The Prisoner'.
Please find brief answers in section: **answers to questions**.

CHAPTER 3

Extract

The ledge, where I placed my candle, had a few mildewed books piled up in one corner; and it was covered with writing scratched on the paint. This writing, however, was nothing but a name repeated in all kinds of characters, large and small—Catherine Earnshaw, here and there varied to Catherine Heathcliff, and then again to Catherine Linton.

In vapid listlessness I leant my head against the window, and continued spelling over Catherine Earnshaw—Heathcliff—Linton, till my eyes closed; but they had not rested five minutes when a glare of white letters started from the dark, as vivid as spectres—the air swarmed with Catherines; and rousing myself to dispel the obtrusive name, I discovered my candle-wick reclining on one of the antique volumes, and perfuming the place with an odour of roasted calf-skin. I snuffed it off, and, very ill at ease under the influence of cold and lingering nausea, sat up and spread open the injured tome on my knee. It was a Testament, in lean type, and smelling dreadfully musty: a fly-leaf bore the inscription—'Catherine Earnshaw, her book,' and a date some quarter of a century back. I shut it, and took up another and another, till I had examined all. Catherine's library was select, and its state of dilapidation proved it to have been well used, though not altogether for a legitimate purpose: scarcely one chapter had escaped, a pen-and-ink commentary—at least the appearance of one—covering every morsel of blank that the printer had left. Some were detached sentences; other parts took the form of a regular diary, scrawled in an unformed, childish hand. At the top of an extra page (quite a treasure, probably, when first lighted on) I was greatly amused to behold an excellent caricature of my friend Joseph,—rudely, yet powerfully sketched. An immediate interest kindled within me for the unknown Catherine, and I began forthwith to decipher her faded hieroglyphics.

'An awful Sunday,' commenced the paragraph beneath. 'I wish my father were back again. Hindley is a detestable substitute—his conduct to Heathcliff is atrocious—H. and I are going to rebel—we took our initiatory step this evening.

Analysis: Brontë creates a real sense of poignancy and emotion with this scene. Lockwood's discovery of Catherine's diary makes us realise that we have been too quick to judge Heathcliff: the diary reveals that he was treated very badly as a child. Thus Brontë begins to establish a major theme of the novel: the way in which the child shapes the man.

Discussion point: Why do children write diaries? Why do you think Brontë establishes Catherine as a character who writes a diary?

Extract

This time, I remembered I was lying in the oak closet, and I heard distinctly the gusty wind, and the driving of the snow; I heard, also, the fir bough repeat its teasing sound, and ascribed it to the right cause: but it annoyed me so much, that I resolved to silence it, if possible; and, I thought, I rose and endeavoured to unhasp the casement. The hook was soldered into the staple: a circumstance observed by me when awake, but forgotten. 'I must stop it, nevertheless!' I muttered, knocking my knuckles through the glass, and stretching an arm out to seize the importunate branch; instead of which, my fingers closed on the fingers of a little, ice-cold hand! The intense horror of nightmare came over me: I tried to draw back my arm, but the hand clung to it, and a most melancholy voice sobbed, 'Let me in—let me in!' 'Who are you?' I asked, struggling, meanwhile, to disengage myself. 'Catherine Linton,' it replied, shiveringly (why did I think of Linton? I had read Earnshaw twenty times for Linton)—'I'm come home: I'd lost my way on the moor!' As it spoke, I discerned, obscurely, a child's face looking through the window. Terror made me cruel; and, finding it useless to attempt shaking the creature off, I pulled its wrist on to the broken pane, and rubbed it to and fro till the blood ran down and soaked the bedclothes: still it wailed, 'Let me in!' and maintained its tenacious gripe, almost maddening me with fear. 'How can I!' I said at length. 'Let me go, if you want me to let you in!' The fingers relaxed, I snatched mine through the hole, hurriedly piled the books up in a pyramid against it, and stopped my ears to exclude the lamentable prayer. I seemed to keep them closed above a quarter of an hour; yet, the instant I listened again, there was the doleful cry moaning on! 'Begone!' I shouted. 'I'll never let you in, not if you beg for twenty years.' 'It is twenty years,' mourned the voice: 'twenty years. I've been a waif for twenty years!'

Analysis: This is perhaps the most famous scene in the novel: the ghost of Cathy trying to get into Wuthering Heights. It introduces a supernatural element into the narrative which haunts and suffuses the rest of the novel. Fascinatingly though, very little of the rest of the novel includes many ghostly qualities. The scene is placed here to create a sense of horror and pathos. Unlike many Gothic novels, Brontë is not interested in establishing a ghostly world – or a real sense of threat from the ghosts. Instead the ghost of Cathy is here as pathetic figures who will never leave: there is no solution to the problem of her haunting. The living are much more to be feared than the dead. A recurrent theme of the book is the pleasures of being dead: it is something that Heathcliff yearns for at the end of the book.

Discussion point: How does Brontë create a real sense of horror and pathos here? Why is this scene so dramatic?

Extract

'Delightful company!' muttered Heathcliff. 'Take the candle, and go where you please. I shall join you directly. Keep out of the yard, though, the dogs are unchained; and the house—Juno mounts sentinel there, and— nay, you can only ramble about the steps and passages. But, away with you! I'll come in two minutes!'

I obeyed, so far as to quit the chamber; when, ignorant where the narrow lobbies led, I stood still, and was witness, involuntarily, to a piece of superstition on the part of my landlord which belied, oddly, his apparent sense. He got on to the bed, and wrenched open the lattice, bursting, as he pulled at it, into an uncontrollable passion of tears. 'Come in! come in!' he sobbed. 'Cathy, do come. Oh, do—once more! Oh! my heart's darling! hear me this time, Catherine, at last!' The spectre showed a spectre's ordinary caprice: it gave no sign of being; but the snow and wind whirled wildly through, even reaching my station, and blowing out the light.

Analysis: Brontë presents us with a very different face of Heathcliff here: he is no longer the sullen, sarcastic, omnipotent ruler of Wuthering Heights, but a love-lorn man desperate for the ghost to come back and haunt him.

Discussion point: How does Brontë generate sympathy for Heathcliff here?

Questions

What is special about the bed that Lockwood finds?
What names are scratched on the window sill?
What is the name inside the Bible?
What is scrawled in the margins of the books?
What does Lockwood dream when he falls asleep?
Why does he wake?
What happens in his second dream?
How does he wake?
What is Heathcliff's response when Lockwood tells him about his dream?
What does 'flaysome' mean? Who is 'owd Nick'?
Devise a **visual organizer** of the key events/literary techniques in the chapter.
GCSE style question: how does Brontë create a sense of the supernatural in this chapter?
GCSE style question: How does the author present dreams in this chapter?
A Level style question: compare and contrast the presentation of the supernatural in this novel with other relevant literature.
Creative response: write a poem/story called 'Strange dreams'.
Please find brief answers in section: **answers to questions**.

CHAPTER 4

Extract

'Well, Mrs. Dean, it will be a charitable deed to tell me something of my neighbours: I feel I shall not rest if I go to bed; so be good enough to sit and chat an hour.'

'Oh, certainly, sir! I'll just fetch a little sewing, and then I'll sit as long as you please. But you've caught cold: I saw you shivering, and you must have some gruel to drive it out.'

The worthy woman bustled off, and I crouched nearer the fire; my head felt hot, and the rest of me chill: moreover, I was excited, almost to a pitch of foolishness, through my nerves and brain. This caused me to feel, not uncomfortable, but rather fearful (as I am still) of serious effects from the incidents of to-day and yesterday. She returned presently, bringing a smoking basin and a basket of work; and, having placed the former on the hob, drew in her seat, evidently pleased to find me so companionable.

Analysis: Lockwood's return to Thrushcross Grange and his subsequent illness lead him to talk more to Nelly Dean. He realises that she holds the secrets of Wuthering Heights in her mind. Thus Brontë shows us how it is the servants in the story who are the most powerful and omniscient people: Zillah wickedly placed Lockwood in Cathy's room, and Nelly is definitely the person with the most knowledge, often engineering, from behind the scenes as it were, the major events of the novel.

Discussion point: Why do you think that Brontë made Nelly the major narrator of the novel?

Extract

This was Heathcliff's first introduction to the family. On coming back a few days afterwards (for I did not consider my banishment perpetual), I found they had christened him 'Heathcliff': it was the name of a son who died in childhood, and it has served him ever since, both for Christian and surname. Miss Cathy and he were now very thick; but Hindley hated him: and to say the truth I did the same; and we plagued and went on with him shamefully: for I wasn't reasonable enough to feel my injustice, and the mistress never put in a word on his behalf when she saw him wronged.

He seemed a sullen, patient child; hardened, perhaps, to ill-treatment: he would stand Hindley's blows without winking or shedding a tear, and my pinches moved him only to draw in a breath and open his eyes, as if he had hurt himself by accident, and nobody was to blame. This endurance made old Earnshaw furious, when he discovered his son persecuting the poor fatherless child, as he called him.

Analysis: The arrival of Heathcliff in 1771, some twenty years before, is effectively the central event of the novel: without Heathcliff there would be no narrative. He is the defining character who appears to shape much of the action. While Nelly, Cathy, Hindley and Hareton will all play some part in shaping the action of the novel, it is Heathcliff's arrival, his love for Cathy and his subsequent thirst for revenge which will create most of the action in the novel. Here, Nelly's description of Heathcliff introduces another major theme: that of prejudice. It is clear from Nelly's use of adjectives to describe Heathcliff – 'dirty, ragged, black-haired, sullen, hardened' – that she disliked him because he seemed so foreign. It is a prejudice which is not shared by the elderly Earnshaw, who, for reasons we never learn, adores the child.

Discussion point: How and why does Brontë introduce the theme of prejudice at this point in the novel? Why does Brontë never reveal the reasons why Earnshaw brought Heathcliff home?

Questions

Why does he ask Mrs Dean about the family at Wuthering Heights?
What does she tell him?
What do we learn about Heathcliff's childhood?
Who resented Heathcliff, how old were they and what did they do to him?
What happened to Heathcliff and Catherine?
Why did Nelly warm to Heathcliff?
GCSE style question: how is Heathcliff presented in this chapter? Why do you think the author presents him as a victim?
A Level style question: compare and contrast the presentation of Heathcliff with a similar character in a relevant text.
Creative response: write a poem/story called 'Bullied'.
Please find brief answers in section: **answers to questions**.

CHAPTER 5

Questions

Who does Earnshaw like the most before he dies?
What does Hindley feel?
How does old Earnshaw treat Catherine and why?
How do Catherine and Heathcliff respond to old Earnshaw's death?
What does Nelly do when she sees the children so upset?
What does Nelly think of the children when she returns?
How does the author and Nelly, the narrator, present Catherine in this chapter?
GCSE style question: how is Heathcliff and Catherine's relationship presented in this chapter?
A Level style question: compare and contrast representations of children in this text with another relevant one.
Creative response: write a poem/story called 'Resentment'.
Please find brief answers in section: **answers to questions**.

CHAPTER 6

Extract

Mr. Hindley came home to the funeral; and—a thing that amazed us, and set the neighbours gossiping right and left—he brought a wife with him. What she was, and where she was born, he never informed us: probably, she had neither money nor name to recommend her, or he would scarcely have kept the union from his father.

Analysis: A few years after Heathcliff arrives at the house, Earnshaw dies. Hindley, who has been at college, and has hated his father for his love of Heathcliff, now returns with a wife to claim his property. Thus Brontë now introduces the next major theme: that of inheritance. Hindley now owns Wuthering Heights and everything in it – including Heathcliff. He sets about gaining his revenge for the ills which he perceived were visited upon him as a child. The childhood idyll that Heathcliff and Cathy have enjoyed has come to an end. It is the end of an era.

Discussion point: How does Brontë build a real sense of suspense here?

Extract

'Where is Miss Catherine?' I cried hurriedly. 'No accident, I hope?' 'At Thrushcross Grange,' he answered; 'and I would have been there too, but they had not the manners to ask me to stay.' 'Well, you will catch it!' I said: 'you'll never be content till you're sent about your business. What in the world led you wandering to Thrushcross Grange?' 'Let me get off my wet clothes, and I'll tell you all about it, Nelly,' he replied. I bid him beware of rousing the master, and while he undressed and I waited to put out the candle, he continued—'Cathy and I escaped from the wash-house to have a ramble at liberty, and getting a glimpse of the Grange lights, we thought we would just go and see whether the Lintons passed their Sunday evenings standing shivering in corners, while their father and mother sat eating and drinking, and singing and laughing, and burning their eyes out before the fire.

Analysis: Heathcliff's escape with Cathy onto the moors and their subsequent adventure at the Grange heralds the first time that the two of them are separated. Life is much changed for Heathcliff who now is banished to the servants' quarters and has his access to Cathy restricted. However, they are still together when they escape onto the moors.

Discussion point: How does Brontë make us feel real sympathy for Cathy and Heathcliff at this point in the novel? Why does their relationship become even more intense? What do the moors represent for them?

Extract

'I told you we laughed,' he answered. 'The Lintons heard us, and with one accord they shot like arrows to the door; there was silence, and then a cry, "Oh, mamma, mamma! Oh, papa! Oh, mamma, come here. Oh, papa, oh!" They really did howl out something in that way. We made frightful noises to terrify them still more, and then we dropped off the ledge, because somebody was drawing the bars, and we felt we had better flee. I had Cathy by the hand, and was urging her on, when all at once she fell down. "Run, Heathcliff, run!" she whispered. "They have let the bull-dog loose, and he holds me!" The devil had seized her ankle, Nelly: I heard his abominable snorting. She did not yell out—no! she would have scorned to do it, if she had been spitted on the horns of a mad cow. I did, though: I vociferated curses enough to annihilate any fiend in Christendom; and I got a stone and thrust it between his jaws, and tried with all my might to cram it down his throat. A beast of a servant came up with a lantern, at last, shouting—"Keep fast, Skulker, keep fast!" He changed his note, however, when he saw Skulker's game. The dog was throttled off; his huge, purple tongue hanging half a foot out of his mouth, and his pendent lips streaming with bloody slaver. The man took Cathy up; she was sick: not from fear, I'm certain, but from pain. He carried her in; I followed, grumbling execrations and vengeance. "What prey, Robert?" hallooed Linton from the entrance. "Skulker has caught a little girl, sir," he replied; "and there's a lad here," he added, making a clutch at me, "who looks an out-and-outer! Very like the robbers were for putting them through the window to open the doors to the gang after all were asleep, that they might murder us at their ease. Hold your tongue, you foul-mouthed thief, you! you shall go to the gallows for this. Mr. Linton, sir, don't lay by your gun." "No, no, Robert," said the old fool. "The rascals knew that yesterday was my rent-day: they thought to have me cleverly. Come in; I'll furnish them a reception. There, John, fasten the chain. Give Skulker some water, Jenny. To beard a magistrate in his stronghold, and on the Sabbath, too! Where will their insolence stop? Oh, my dear Mary, look here! Don't be afraid, it is but a boy—yet the villain scowls so plainly in his face; would it not be a kindness to the country to hang him at once, before he shows his nature in acts as well as features?" He pulled me under the chandelier, and Mrs. Linton placed her spectacles on her nose and raised her hands in horror. The cowardly children crept nearer also, Isabella lisping—"Frightful thing! Put him in the cellar, papa. He's exactly like the son of the fortune-teller that stole my tame pheasant. Isn't he, Edgar?"

'While they examined me, Cathy came round; she heard the last speech, and laughed. Edgar Linton, after an inquisitive stare, collected sufficient wit to recognise her.

Analysis: Heathcliff and Cathy had been laughing at Isabella and her brother Edgar arguing over their pet dog, but then have a more savage dog set upon them when they are heard. Heathcliff bravely tries to rescue Cathy but cannot. We gain a sense of a world where the wealthy feel very insecure: the bulldog is unleashed at the first sign that there might be intruders. Compare this with Lockwood's treatment at Wuthering Heights: he may not be welcome but he is not attacked!

Discussion point: How does Brontë make this such a dramatic scene?

Questions

Who does Hindley return with after the funeral?

What job does Hindley give Heathcliff and how does he restrict him?

How do Catherine and Heathcliff escape from Hindley's bullying?

What does Heathcliff tell Nelly one evening?

How does Mr Linton tell off Hindley?

What is the effect of the different narrators in this chapter?

GCSE style question: how does the author build sympathy for Heathcliff?

A Level style question: how are the places of Thrushcross Grange and Wuthering Heights similar and different in this chapter?

Creative response: write a poem/story called 'Nice and nasty' about two different people and/or places, exploring some of the themes in this chapter.

Please find brief answers in section: **answers to questions**.

CHAPTER 7

Extract

Cathy stayed at Thrushcross Grange five weeks: till Christmas. By that time her ankle was thoroughly cured, and her manners much improved. The mistress visited her often in the interval, and commenced her plan of reform by trying to raise her self-respect with fine clothes and flattery, which she took readily; so that, instead of a wild, hatless little savage jumping into the house, and rushing to squeeze us all breathless, there 'lighted from a handsome black pony a very dignified person, with brown ringlets falling from the cover of a feathered beaver, and a long cloth habit, which she was obliged to hold up with both hands that she might sail in.

Analysis: Here we see the transformation of Cathy. She becomes aware of her own social status at Thrushcross Grange in a way she never was at Wuthering Heights. Thus it appears that the two houses represent the two sides of the English middle-classes: we have the rough brutality of the farming middle class, who care little for social conventions, and the gentility of the Linton family. Previously, she was a wild savage, but now she is a dignified person.

Discussion point: How and why does Brontë create suspense and drama in Cathy's transformation?

Extract

'Nay, sir,' I could not avoid answering, 'he'll touch nothing, not he: and I suppose he must have his share of the dainties as well as we.'

'He shall have his share of my hand, if I catch him downstairs till dark,' cried Hindley. 'Begone, you vagabond! What! you are attempting the coxcomb, are you? Wait till I get hold of those elegant locks—see if I won't pull them a bit longer!'

'They are long enough already,' observed Master Linton, peeping from the doorway; 'I wonder they don't make his head ache. It's like a colt's mane over his eyes!'

He ventured this remark without any intention to insult; but Heathcliff's violent nature was not prepared to endure the appearance of impertinence from one whom he seemed to hate, even then, as a rival. He seized a tureen of hot apple sauce (the first thing that came under his gripe) and dashed it full against the speaker's face and neck; who instantly commenced a lament that brought Isabella and Catherine hurrying to the place. Mr. Earnshaw snatched up the culprit directly and conveyed him to his chamber; where, doubtless, he administered a rough remedy to cool the fit of passion, for he appeared red and breathless.

Analysis: Heathcliff's violent attack upon the civilised Linton is very shocking, but we can sympathise with him by now.

Discussion point: How and why does the reader have sympathy for Heathcliff at this point in the novel? What is our attitude towards Linton?

Extract

Catherine loved it too: but she said it sounded sweetest at the top of the steps, and she went up in the dark: I followed. They shut the house door below, never noting our absence, it was so full of people. She made no stay at the stairs'-head, but mounted farther, to the garret where Heathcliff was confined, and called him. He stubbornly declined answering for a while: she persevered, and finally persuaded him to hold communion with her through the boards. I let the poor things converse unmolested, till I supposed the songs were going to cease, and the singers to get some refreshment: then I clambered up the ladder to warn her. Instead of finding her outside, I heard her voice within. The little monkey had crept by the skylight of one garret, along the roof, into the skylight of the other, and it was with the utmost difficulty I could coax her out again. When she did come, Heathcliff came with her, and she insisted that I should take him into the kitchen, as my fellow-servant had gone to a neighbour's, to be removed from the sound of our 'devil's psalmody,' as it pleased him to call it. I told them I intended by no means to encourage their tricks: but as the prisoner had never broken his fast since yesterday's dinner, I would wink at his cheating Mr. Hindley that once. He went down: I set him a stool by the fire, and offered him a quantity of good things: but he was sick and could eat little, and my attempts to entertain him were thrown away. He leant his two elbows on his knees, and his chin on his hands and remained rapt in dumb meditation. On my inquiring the subject of his thoughts, he answered gravely—'I'm trying to settle how I shall pay Hindley back. I don't care how long I wait, if I can only do it at last. I hope he will not die before I do!'

Analysis: Heathcliff's vow here is one which will inform much of the action in the novel: from this point onwards the novel becomes a 'revenger's tragedy'.

Discussion point: Why does Heathcliff want revenge? How does Brontë create suspense here?

Questions

How long does Catherine stay at the Grange?
How has Heathcliff been treated?
Why is Heathcliff upset by Catherine?
How does Heathcliff make a big effort for Catherine?
What does Edgar say about Heathcliff's appearance?
What is Heathcliff's response and what does Hindley do?
What does Catherine do to help Heathcliff?
What does Heathcliff promise to do?
GCSE style question: how does the author present the themes of social justice and ambition in this chapter?
A Level style question: compare and contrast the way in which this novel explores social justice with another text of your choice.
Creative response: write a poem/story called 'Unfair'.
Please find brief answers in section: **answers to questions**.

CHAPTER 8

Extract

On the morning of a fine June day my first bonny little nursling, and the last of the ancient Earnshaw stock, was born. We were busy with the hay in a far-away field, when the girl that usually brought our breakfasts came running an hour too soon across the meadow and up the lane, calling me as she ran.

'Oh, such a grand bairn!' she panted out. 'The finest lad that ever breathed! But the doctor says missis must go: he says she's been in a consumption these many months. I heard him tell Mr. Hindley: and now she has nothing to keep her, and she'll be dead before winter. You must come home directly. You're to nurse it, Nelly: to feed it with sugar and milk, and take care of it day and night. I wish I were you, because it will be all yours when there is no missis!'

Analysis: The birth of Hareton heralds the arrival of a new generation: a generation which will be central to the second half of the book. It is also introduces a major theme: that of childbirth killing off mothers. The death of his wife, Frances, drives Hindley to despair and drink: his treatment of Heathcliff becomes even more brutal.

Discussion point: Why does Brontë kill off so many mothers in this book?

Extract

'Cathy, are you busy this afternoon?' asked Heathcliff. 'Are you going anywhere?'

'No, it is raining,' she answered.

'Why have you that silk frock on, then?' he said. 'Nobody coming here, I hope?'

'Not that I know of,' stammered Miss: 'but you should be in the field now, Heathcliff. It is an hour past dinnertime: I thought you were gone.'

'Hindley does not often free us from his accursed presence,' observed the boy. 'I'll not work any more to-day: I'll stay with you.'

'Oh, but Joseph will tell,' she suggested; 'you'd better go!'

'Joseph is loading lime on the further side of Penistone Crags; it will take him till dark, and he'll never know.'

So, saying, he lounged to the fire, and sat down. Catherine reflected an instant, with knitted brows—she found it needful to smooth the way for an intrusion. 'Isabella and Edgar Linton talked of calling this afternoon,' she said, at the conclusion of a minute's silence. 'As it rains, I hardly expect them; but they may come, and if they do, you run the risk of being scolded for no good.'

'Order Ellen to say you are engaged, Cathy,' he persisted; 'don't turn me out for those pitiful, silly friends of yours!

Analysis: Heathcliff becomes offended when he sees Cathy putting on a 'silly frock' to please Edgar, who is coming to visit. He now begs her not to see Edgar.

Discussion point: How does Brontë create sympathy for Heathcliff here?

Extract

Little Hareton, who followed me everywhere, and was sitting near me on the floor, at seeing my tears commenced crying himself, and sobbed out complaints against 'wicked aunt Cathy,' which drew her fury on to his unlucky head: she seized his shoulders, and shook him till the poor child waxed livid, and Edgar thoughtlessly laid hold of her hands to deliver him. In an instant one was wrung free, and the astonished young man felt it applied over his own ear in a way that could not be mistaken for jest. He drew back in consternation. I lifted Hareton in my arms, and walked off to the kitchen with him, leaving the door of communication open, for I was curious to watch how they would settle their disagreement. The insulted visitor moved to the spot where he had laid his hat, pale and with a quivering lip.

'That's right!' I said to myself. 'Take warning and begone! It's a kindness to let you have a glimpse of her genuine disposition.'

'Where are you going?' demanded Catherine, advancing to the door.

He swerved aside, and attempted to pass.

'You must not go!' she exclaimed, energetically.

'I must and shall!' he replied in a subdued voice.

'No,' she persisted, grasping the handle; 'not yet, Edgar Linton: sit down; you shall not leave me in that temper. I should be miserable all night, and I won't be miserable for you!'

Analysis: We now see another side to Cathy who has unreasonably nipped Nelly and hit Edgar, much to his surprise. She is not the lady that Edgar imagined her to be. However, he is so besotted with her that the incident actually brings them closer together: they profess themselves lovers after this.

Discussion point: What do you think of Brontë's characterisation of Cathy here? What is Brontë saying about love here?

Questions

What happens to Hindley's wife? What is Hindley's response?

What problem does Catherine have?

What does Catherine criticise Heathcliff for?

How does the relationship between Edgar and Catherine develop?

How does the author present Catherine in this chapter?

GCSE style question: how is imagery used in this chapter?

A Level style question: compare and contrast the ways in which Brontë and another author deploy animalistic imagery.

Creative response: write a story/poem called 'Jealousy'.

Please find brief answers in section: **answers to questions**.

CHAPTER 9

Extract

'Why do you love him, Miss Cathy?'
'Nonsense, I do—that's sufficient.'

'By no means; you must say why?'

'Well, because he is handsome, and pleasant to be with.'

'Bad!' was my commentary.

'And because he is young and cheerful.'

'Bad, still.'

'And because he loves me.'

'Indifferent, coming there.'

'And he will be rich, and I shall like to be the greatest woman of the neighbourhood, and I shall be proud of having such a husband.'

'Worst of all. And now, say how you love him?'

'As everybody loves—You're silly, Nelly.'

'Not at all—Answer.'

'I love the ground under his feet, and the air over his head, and everything he touches, and every word he says. I love all his looks, and all his actions, and him entirely and altogether. There now!'

'And why?'

'Nay; you are making a jest of it: it is exceedingly ill-natured! It's no jest to me!' said the young lady, scowling, and turning her face to the fire.

'I'm very far from jesting, Miss Catherine,' I replied. 'You love Mr. Edgar because he is handsome, and young, and cheerful, and rich, and loves you. The last, however, goes for nothing: you would love him without that, probably; and with it you wouldn't, unless he possessed the four former attractions.'

'No, to be sure not: I should only pity him—hate him, perhaps, if he were ugly, and a clown.'

'But there are several other handsome, rich young men in the world: handsomer, possibly, and richer than he is. What should hinder you from loving them?'

'If there be any, they are out of my way: I've seen none like Edgar.'

Analysis: This discussion takes place in the context of Hindley's drunken rages: the atmosphere in the house is becoming insufferable. Hindley has nearly killed his son Hareton in a fit of anger: only Heathcliff's intervention saves the little boy. We now see Cathy looking for ways out of this situation. Here she is talking to Nelly about her feelings for Linton, making it clear that his wealth is important to her. We also see how Nelly has become an important person to both Heathcliff and Cathy, as well as a surrogate mother to Hareton.

Discussion point: What do you think of Cathy's attitude towards Linton?

Extract

'If I were in heaven, Nelly, I should be extremely miserable.'

'Because you are not fit to go there,' I answered. 'All sinners would be miserable in heaven.'

'But it is not for that. I dreamt once that I was there.'

'I tell you I won't hearken to your dreams, Miss Catherine! I'll go to bed,' I interrupted again.

She laughed, and held me down; for I made a motion to leave my chair.

'This is nothing,' cried she: 'I was only going to say that heaven did not seem to be my home; and I broke my heart with weeping to come back to earth; and the angels were so angry that they flung me out into the middle of the heath on the top of Wuthering Heights; where I woke sobbing for joy. That will do to explain my secret, as well as the other. I've no more business to marry Edgar Linton than I have to be in heaven; and if the wicked man in there had not brought Heathcliff so low, I shouldn't have thought of it. It would degrade me to marry Heathcliff now; so he shall never know how I love him: and that, not because he's handsome, Nelly, but because he's more myself than I am. Whatever our souls are made of, his and mine are the same; and Linton's is as different as a moonbeam from lightning, or frost from fire.'

Ere this speech ended I became sensible of Heathcliff's presence. Having noticed a slight movement, I turned my head, and saw him rise from the bench, and steal out noiselessly. He had listened till he heard Catherine say it would degrade her to marry him, and then he stayed to hear no further. My companion, sitting on the ground, was prevented by the back of the settle from remarking his presence or departure; but I started, and bade her hush!

Analysis: This is a crucial turning point in the novel. After learning that Cathy will never marry him because it would 'degrade' her, he departs. Many critics have noted that Catherine's speeches have such a powerful poetry about them that the reader is sucked into colluding and possibly agreeing with the terrible things she says and does. The rhythm of this speech is powered by the use of alliteration, which occurs in page after page of the novel. Here the alliterating words are: "heaven", "home", "hearth", and, of course, "Heights". These 'H' words are carefully placed throughout the novel, particularly in Brontë's use of names: Hindley, Hareton, Heathcliff. Thus Brontë is both able to suggest through the repetition of the 'H' how these characters are both related in nature, similar in some respects, but different in others. The 'H' suggests passion, strength and love – all qualities that these characters exhibit – but also it connotes abuse, neglect, victimhood. Some critics have gone so far as to say that Brontë makes her use of language like music in its use of repeated consonant sounds to create atmosphere and suggest character. In the above speech, we see how Catherine does not wish to be with God in heaven, but instead wants to be in the 'earth...the middle of the heath'. This is her original home because it takes her back to Heathcliff. Yet, Heathcliff is socially inferior to Linton and therefore she can't marry him: the forces of society, not nature prevail with Catherine. For all her passionate, pagan poetry about wanting to amidst the wilds of nature, she has been civilised too much. Thus we see how Emily reveals the corrupting nature of society, which is in contrast to the truth of nature, which is where her true soul is.

Discussion point: How and why does Brontë make this speech such a dramatic and poetic moment in the novel?

Extract

Much against my inclination, I was persuaded to leave Wuthering Heights and accompany her here. Little Hareton was nearly five years old, and I had just begun to teach him his letters. We made a sad parting; but Catherine's tears were more powerful than ours. When I refused to go, and when she found her entreaties did not move me, she went lamenting to her husband and brother. The former offered me munificent wages; the latter ordered me to pack up: he wanted no women in the house, he said, now that there was no mistress; and as to Hareton, the curate should take him in hand, by-and-by. And so I had but one choice left: to do as I was ordered. I told the master he got rid of all decent people only to run to ruin a little faster; I kissed Hareton, said good-by; and since then he has been a stranger: and it's very queer to think it, but I've no doubt he has completely forgotten all about Ellen Dean, and that he was ever more than all the world to her and she to him!

Analysis: Cathy marries Edgar after Heathcliff disappears in a storm. It is the end of an era: the childhood sweethearts are separated, Cathy is now a respectable married woman, and Nelly has to leave her surrogate child, Hareton.

Discussion point: How does Brontë keep the reader wondering what will happen next? What mysteries and possible conflicts lie ahead?

* * * * *

At this point of the housekeeper's story she chanced to glance towards the time-piece over the chimney; and was in amazement on seeing the minute-hand measure half-past one. She would not hear of staying a second longer: in truth, I felt rather disposed to defer the sequel of her narrative myself. And now that she is vanished to her rest, and I have meditated for another hour or two, I shall summon courage to go also, in spite of aching laziness of head and limbs.

Questions

How does Heathcliff save Hareton?
What does Catherine tell Nelly?
What dream does Catherine tell Nelly about?
Why won't she marry Heathcliff?

Who is listening and what is the listener's response?

What doesn't he hear Catherine say?

What does Catherine do when she realises who was listening?

What happens after that?

GCSE style question: how are Catherine's feelings represented in this chapter?

A Level style question: compare and contrast the representation of women in this novel with another text of your choice.

Creative response: write a story/poem called 'The Love Triangle'.

Please find brief answers in section: **answers to questions**.

CHAPTER 10

Extract

She quitted the apartment; Mr. Edgar inquired, carelessly, who it was.

'Some one mistress does not expect,' I replied. 'That Heathcliff—you recollect him, sir—who used to live at Mr. Earnshaw's.'

'What! the gipsy—the ploughboy?' he cried. 'Why did you not say so to Catherine?'

'Hush! you must not call him by those names, master,' I said. 'She'd be sadly grieved to hear you. She was nearly heartbroken when he ran off. I guess his return will make a jubilee to her.'

Mr. Linton walked to a window on the other side of the room that overlooked the court. He unfastened it, and leant out. I suppose they were below, for he exclaimed quickly: 'Don't stand there, love! Bring the person in, if it be anyone particular.' Ere long, I heard the click of the latch, and Catherine flew up-stairs, breathless and wild; too excited to show gladness: indeed, by her face, you would rather have surmised an awful calamity.

'Oh, Edgar, Edgar!' she panted, flinging her arms round his neck. 'Oh, Edgar darling! Heathcliff's come back—he is!' And she tightened her embrace to a squeeze.

'Well, well,' cried her husband, crossly, 'don't strangle me for that! He never struck me as such a marvellous treasure. There is no need to be frantic!'

Analysis: The return of Heathcliff is conveyed in dialogue. It is a breathless, excited event – and a real narrative surprise.

Discussion point: What does the dialogue reveal about Cathy and Edgar's marriage and their attitudes towards Heathcliff?

Extract

He took a seat opposite Catherine, who kept her gaze fixed on him as if she feared he would vanish were she to remove it. He did not raise his to her often: a quick glance now and then sufficed; but it flashed back time more confidently, the undisguised delight he drank from hers. were too much absorbed in their mutual joy to suffer embarrassment. ɪ so Mr. Edgar: he grew pale with pure annoyance: a feeling that reached iι climax when his lady rose, and stepping across the rug, seized Heathcliff's hands again, and laughed like one beside herself.

'I shall think it a dream to-morrow!' she cried. 'I shall not be able to believe that I have seen, and touched, and spoken to you once more. And yet, cruel Heathcliff! you don't deserve this welcome. To be absent and silent for three years, and never to think of me!'

Analysis: The transformation of Heathcliff is another great surprise. Instead being defeated by the outside world, it appears that he has triumphed. We never learn the reason why he has become so wealthy and such a formidable figure.

Discussion point: What do you think happened to Heathcliff during the three years he was away?

Extract

'You are an impertinent little monkey!' exclaimed Mrs. Linton, in surprise. 'But I'll not believe this idiotcy! It is impossible that you can covet the admiration of Heathcliff—that you consider him an agreeable person! I hope I have misunderstood you, Isabella?'

'No, you have not,' said the infatuated girl. 'I love him more than ever you loved Edgar, and he might love me, if you would let him!'

'I wouldn't be you for a kingdom, then!' Catherine declared, emphatically: and she seemed to speak sincerely. 'Nelly, help me to convince her of her madness. Tell her what Heathcliff is: an unreclaimed creature, without refinement, without cultivation; an arid wilderness of furze and whinstone. I'd as soon put that little canary into the park on a winter's day, as recommend you to bestow your heart on him! It is deplorable ignorance of his character, child, and nothing else, which makes that dream enter your head. Pray, don't imagine that he conceals depths of benevolence and affection beneath a stern exterior! He's not a rough diamond—a pearl-containing oyster of a rustic: he's a fierce, pitiless, wolfish man. I never say to him, "Let this or that enemy alone, because it would be ungenerous or cruel to harm them;" I say, "Let them alone, because I should hate them to be wronged:" and he'd crush you like a sparrow's egg, Isabella, if he found you a troublesome charge.

Analysis: Brontë creates real tension in the way Isabella becomes infatuated with Heathcliff. The eighteen-year-old is jealous that Cathy spends too much time with him. To give her due, Cathy warns Isabella that Heathcliff is a very bad person to fall in love with.

n point: How does Brontë create tension in her
the triangular relationship between Isabella, Cathy

_ns_

. nappens after Catherine and Edgar have been married for six
_onths?

Why is Edgar surprised?

Why is Edgar troubled by Catherine?

What happens to Isabella?

Why is she annoyed with Catherine?

What does Catherine do to get her own back on Isabella?

What is Heathcliff's attitude towards Isabella?

How does Nelly show her loyalty to Edgar?

What do you think happened to Heathcliff while he was away? Why does the author leave it a mystery, do you think?

GCSE style question: how does the author build a sense of threat and foreboding in this chapter?

GCSE style question: how is the relationship between Edgar and Catherine represented in this chapter? What has ruined their chance of happiness, according to Nelly?

A Level style question: compare and contrast the representation of marriage in this text with another relevant text.

Creative response: write a poem/story called 'Marriage'.

Please find brief answers in section: **answers to questions**.

CHAPTER 11

Extract

'Who has taught you those fine words, my bairn?' I inquired. 'The curate?'

'Damn the curate, and thee! Gie me that,' he replied.

'Tell us where you got your lessons, and you shall have it,' said I. 'Who's your master?'

'Devil daddy,' was his answer.

'And what do you learn from daddy?' I continued.

He jumped at the fruit; I raised it higher. 'What does he teach you?' I asked.

'Naught,' said he, 'but to keep out of his gait. Daddy cannot bide me, because I swear at him.'

'Ah! and the devil teaches you to swear at daddy?' I observed.

'Ay—nay,' he drawled.

'Who, then?'

'Heathcliff.'

'I asked if he liked Mr. Heathcliff.'

'Ay!' he answered again.

Desiring to have his reasons for liking him, I could only gather the sentences—'I known't: he pays dad back what he gies to me—he curses daddy for cursing me. He says I mun do as I will.'

'And the curate does not teach you to read and write, then?' I pursued.

'No, I was told the curate should have his—teeth dashed down his—throat, if he stepped over the threshold—Heathcliff had promised that!'

Analysis: Nelly visits Wuthering Heights and finds that Hareton is running wild, having learnt some foul language from Heathcliff. Bizarrely though, Hareton has a strong admiration for Heathcliff, perceiving him as his protector: "he pays back what gives to me – he curses daddy for cursing me." Thus we see that Heathcliff in his anxiety to form important alliances to facilitate his revenge against Hindley and Lindon forms friendships in the process too: Isabella becomes besotted with him, and Hareton regards him as a surrogate father.

Discussion point: To what extent is Heathcliff presented as a friend to Hareton and Isabella? To what extent do you think Nelly's negative view of him is biased?

Extract

'Remain where you are, Catherine,' he said; without any anger in his voice, but with much sorrowful despondency. 'I shall not stay. I am neither come to wrangle nor be reconciled; but I wish just to learn whether, after this evening's events, you intend to continue your intimacy with—'

'Oh, for mercy's sake,' interrupted the mistress, stamping her foot, 'for mercy's sake, let us hear no more of it now! Your cold blood cannot be worked into a fever: your veins are full of ice-water; but mine are boiling, and the sight of such chillness makes them dance.'

'To get rid of me, answer my question,' persevered Mr. Linton. 'You must answer it; and that violence does not alarm me. I have found that you can be as stoical as anyone, when you please. Will you give up Heathcliff hereafter, or will you give up me? It is impossible for you to be my friend and his at the same time; and I absolutely require to know which you choose.'

'I require to be let alone!' exclaimed Catherine, furiously. 'I demand it! Don't you see I can scarcely stand? Edgar, you—you leave me!'

Analysis: Finally, Linton snaps and orders Heathcliff to leave, talking about his 'miserable, degraded' character; in other words, Linton is referring to Heathcliff's lowly social status, his tendency to be gloomy, his interest in exploiting people. Heathcliff is a 'moral poison' because he is so persuasive: Linton's own sister, Isabella, is besotted by him, and his wife is in love with him. Notice how

Heathcliff does not even bother to address Linton directly but instead talks to Cathy in a sarcastic fashion, calling Linton a 'lamb' and suggesting that he is not worth hitting. This provokes a furious reaction from the normally placid Linton who hits him. Cathy's reaction is typically passively aggressive: she uses her illness as a way of frightening Linton, of subjugating him.

Discussion point: How does Brontë make this such a dramatic confrontation?

Questions

What does Hareton do to Nelly?
What has Heathcliff taught Hareton to do?
What does Nelly see Heathcliff doing with Isabella?
What does Heathcliff say when Catherine becomes angry with him?
Who tells Edgar what has happened?
Why does Catherine lock Edgar and Heathcliff in a room? What happens to Edgar?
What does Catherine do when Edgar says she must decide him or Heathcliff?
What does Edgar threaten Isabella if she encourages Heathcliff?
GCSE style question: how is Nelly represented in this chapter?
GCSE style question: how does Brontë create a sense of drama and conflict in the chapter?
A Level style question: compare and contrast the representation of alienation in this novel with another text of your choice.
Creative response: write Edgar's diary for this chapter.
Please find brief answers in section: **answers to questions**.

CHAPTER 12

Extract

'Well, it seems a weary number of hours,' she muttered doubtfully: 'it must be more. I remember being in the parlour after they had quarrelled, and Edgar being cruelly provoking, and me running into this room desperate. As soon as ever I had barred the door, utter blackness overwhelmed me, and I fell on the floor. I couldn't explain to Edgar how certain I felt of having a fit, or going raging mad, if he persisted in teasing me! I had no command of tongue, or brain, and he did not guess my agony, perhaps: it barely left me sense to try to escape from him and his voice. Before I recovered sufficiently to see and hear, it began to be dawn, and, Nelly, I'll tell you what I thought, and what has kept recurring and recurring till I feared for my reason. I thought as I lay there, with my head against that table leg, and my eyes dimly discerning the grey square of the window, that I was enclosed in the oak-panelled bed at home; and my heart ached with some great grief which, just waking, I could not recollect. I pondered, and worried myself to discover what it could be, and, most strangely, the whole last seven years of my life grew a blank! I did not recall that they had been at all. I was a child; my father was just buried, and my misery arose from the separation that Hindley had ordered between me and Heathcliff. I was laid alone, for the first time; and, rousing from a dismal doze after a night of weeping, I lifted my hand to push the panels aside: it struck the table-top! I swept it along the carpet, and then memory burst in: my late anguish was swallowed in a paroxysm of despair. I cannot say why I felt so wildly wretched: it must have been temporary derangement; for there is scarcely cause. But, supposing at twelve years old I had been wrenched from the Heights, and every early association, and my all in all, as Heathcliff was at that time, and been converted at a stroke into Mrs. Linton, the lady of Thrushcross Grange, and the wife of a stranger: an exile, and outcast, thenceforth, from what had been my world. You may fancy a glimpse of the abyss where I grovelled! Shake your head as you will, Nelly, you have helped to unsettle me! You should have spoken to Edgar, indeed you should, and compelled him to leave me quiet! Oh, I'm burning! I wish I were out of doors! I wish I were a girl again, half savage and hardy, and free; and laughing at injuries, not maddening under them! Why am I so changed? why does my blood rush into a hell of tumult at a few words? I'm sure I should be myself were I once among the heather on those hills. Open the window again wide: fasten it open! Quick, why don't you move?'

Analysis: Cathy's illness is tempestuous and soaked with regrets and memories. Her raging fever makes her cry out her innermost desires: 'I wish I were a girl again'. Heathcliff has now disappeared, having eloped with Isabella. Her distraught behaviour is clearly linked to Heathcliff's disappearance. She is now realising that her social snobbery has prevented her from leading a happy life and causing tragedy.

Discussion point: What role does illness play in the novel? Why do the characters become sick?

Questions

How long does Catherine refuse food for?
Why does Nelly not tell Edgar about her condition?
What does Catherine imagine in her delirium?
What does Catherine come to realise is the source of her misery?.
Why is Edgar angry with Nelly?
What does Nelly hear about as she goes to fetch the doctor for Catherine?
Why doesn't she tell Edgar?
What does Edgar do when he learns of the elopement?

GCSE style question: how does Brontë present Nelly in this chapter?
GCSE style question: how does Brontë present Catherine in this chapter?
A Level style question: compare and contrast Brontë's presentation of elopement with another relevant text.
Creative response: write a poem/story called 'The Elopement'.
Please find brief answers in section: **answers to questions**.

CHAPTER 13

Extract

Directly after Joseph came up with Hareton, to put him to bed. I had found shelter in Hareton's room, and the old man, on seeing me, said,— 'They's rahm for boath ye un' yer pride, now, I sud think i' the hahse. It's empty; ye may hev' it all to yerseln, un' Him as allus maks a third, i' sich ill company!'

Gladly did I take advantage of this intimation; and the minute I flung myself into a chair, by the fire, I nodded, and slept. My slumber was deep and sweet, though over far too soon. Mr. Heathcliff awoke me; he had just come in, and demanded, in his loving manner, what I was doing there? I told him the cause of my staying up so late—that he had the key of our room in his pocket. The adjective our gave mortal offence. He swore it was not, nor ever should be, mine; and he'd—but I'll not repeat his language, nor describe his habitual conduct: he is ingenious and unresting in seeking to gain my abhorrence! I sometimes wonder at him with an intensity that deadens my fear: yet, I assure you, a tiger or a venomous serpent could not rouse terror in me equal to that which he wakens. He told me of Catherine's illness, and accused my brother of causing it promising that I should be Edgar's proxy in suffering, till he could get hold of him.

I do hate him—I am wretched—I have been a fool! Beware of uttering one breath of this to any one at the Grange. I shall expect you every day—don't disappoint me!—Isabella.

> Analysis: Here we see Edgar's devotion to his errant wife, tending her like a child. We realise that the two of them are locked into a co-dependent relationship: they get on better with each other when Cathy is sick. Isabella's letter reveals that the marriage is utterly wretched.

> Discussion point: What are our feelings towards Isabella and Edgar at this point? How have our feelings towards them changed?

Questions

How long is Catherine ill for and with what?
What does Isabella's letter reveal?

GCSE style question: how does Brontë present Isabella in this chapter?

A Level style question: compare and contrast the presentation of Isabella with a similar character in another text.

Creative response: write a poem/story called 'Deceived'.

Please find brief answers in section: **answers to questions**.

CHAPTER 14

Extract

'There—that will do for the present!' said Heathcliff. 'If you are called upon in a court of law, you'll remember her language, Nelly! And take a good look at that countenance: she's near the point which would suit me. No; you're not fit to be your own guardian, Isabella, now; and I, being your legal protector, must retain you in my custody, however distasteful the obligation may be. Go up-stairs; I have something to say to Ellen Dean in private. That's not the way: up-stairs, I tell you! Why, this is the road upstairs, child!'

He seized, and thrust her from the room; and returned muttering—'I have no pity! I have no pity! The more the worms writhe, the more I yearn to crush out their entrails! It is a moral teething; and I grind with greater energy in proportion to the increase of pain.'

'Do you understand what the word pity means?' I said, hastening to resume my bonnet. 'Did you ever feel a touch of it in your life?'

Analysis: Brontë creates real tension with Heathcliff's return and his insistence upon seeing Cathy, despite the fact that Linton has insisted it must not happen.

Discussion point: What is revealed about Heathcliff and Nelly at this point?

Questions

What does Edgar refuse to do?

What does Nelly find when she visits the Heights?

What does Heathcliff insist upon when he hears about Catherine's illness?

Why does Nelly come to agree to help Heathcliff see Catherine?

Why does Lockwood associate himself with Heathcliff and why is he presented in an ironic light?

GCSE style question: how is Heathcliff presented in this chapter?

A Level style question: compare and contrast the ways in which Brontë and one other writer of your choice presents the theme of pride.

Creative response: write a poem/story called 'The Loser Who Won'.

Please find brief answers in section: **answers to questions**.

CHAPTER 15

Extract

'I shall not be at peace,' moaned Catherine, recalled to a sense of physical weakness by the violent, unequal throbbing of her heart, which beat visibly and audibly under this excess of agitation. She said nothing further till the paroxysm was over; then she continued, more kindly—

'I'm not wishing you greater torment than I have, Heathcliff. I only wish us never to be parted: and should a word of mine distress you hereafter, think I feel the same distress underground, and for my own sake, forgive me! Come here and kneel down again! You never harmed me in your life. Nay, if you nurse anger, that will be worse to remember than my harsh words! Won't you come here again? Do!'

Analysis: This tortuous scene, occurring as it does just before Catherine dies, is notable for the way it portrays Cathy's feelings. Some are clearly utterly fixed: her immoveable love for Heathcliff is clear, but she has mixed feelings about how Heathcliff views her, and almost seems to be toying with him, deliberately torturing him. Cathy is also speculating about the nature of the after-life?

Discussion point: Why do you think Cathy tortures Heathcliff at this point? What are your feelings towards Cathy? What is Cathy's attitude towards the after-life? What do you think of her attitudes towards the after-life?

Questions

When does Nelly give Heathcliff's letter to Catherine?

What does Heathcliff do?

What does Heathcliff realise about Catherine?

What does Catherine accuse Heathcliff of?

What does he accuse her of?

How does their argument end?

What does Heathcliff do when Edgar enters?

GCSE style question: how does the author represent the desire to escape in this chapter?

GCSE style question: how does the author represent the themes of passion and betrayal in this chapter?

A Level style question: compare and contrast Brontë's presentation of passion with another relevant text.

Creative response: write a poem/story called 'The Accusation'.

Please find brief answers in section: **answers to questions**.

CHAPTER 16

Extract

The place of Catherine's interment, to the surprise of the villagers, was neither in the chapel under the carved monument of the Lintons, nor yet by the tombs of her own relations, outside. It was dug on a green slope in a corner of the kirk-yard, where the wall is so low that heath and bilberry-plants have climbed over it from the moor; and peat-mould almost buries it. Her husband lies in the same spot now; and they have each a simple headstone above, and a plain grey block at their feet, to mark the graves.

Analysis: Here we see Heathcliff trying to stifle his true feelings for Cathy after learning from Nelly that she is dead. We later learn that he dashes his head against a tree such is his grief; but here he is keen to suppress his feelings.

Discussion point: Why does Heathcliff suppress his feelings?

Questions

What happens to Catherine that night? Why?

When does Heathcliff realise what has happened to Catherine? Why?

What does he hope Catherine will do?

What does Heathcliff do to Catherine's locket?

What does Nelly do?

Why is it convenient for Heathcliff that Edgar has no son? GCSE style question: how does the author present Heathcliff's trauma in this chapter?

GCSE style question: why is Catherine's grave a fitting place for her? It borders the moor, which she loved to go to with Heathcliff.

A Level style question: compare and contrast Brontë's presentation of death with another relevant text.

Creative response: write Heathcliff's diary for this scene.

Please find brief answers in section: **answers to questions**.

CHAPTER 17

Extract

That Friday made the last of our fine days for a month. In the evening the weather broke: the wind shifted from south to north-east, and brought rain first, and then sleet and snow. On the morrow one could hardly imagine that there had been three weeks of summer: the primroses and crocuses were hidden under wintry drifts; the larks were silent, the young leaves of the early trees smitten and blackened. And dreary, and chill, and dismal, that morrow did creep over! My master kept his room; I took possession of the lonely parlour, converting it into a nursery: and there I was, sitting with the moaning doll of a child laid on my knee; rocking it to and fro, and watching, meanwhile, the still driving flakes build up the uncurtained window, when the door opened, and some person entered, out of breath and laughing! My anger was greater than my astonishment for a minute. I supposed it one of the maids, and I cried—'Have done! How dare you show your giddiness here; What would Mr. Linton say if he heard you?'

'Excuse me!' answered a familiar voice; 'but I know Edgar is in bed, and I cannot stop myself.'

With that the speaker came forward to the fire, panting and holding her hand to her side.

'I have run the whole way from Wuthering Heights!' she continued, after a pause; 'except where I've flown. I couldn't count the number of falls I've had. Oh, I'm aching all over! Don't be alarmed! There shall be an explanation as soon as I can give it; only just have the goodness to step out and order the carriage to take me on to Gimmerton, and tell a servant to seek up a few clothes in my wardrobe.'

Analysis: Isabella escapes from Wuthering Heights, telling a harrowing tale of her imprisonment.

Discussion point: What do you think of Isabella at this point in the novel? How have your attitudes changed?

Extract

'Well,' said the scoundrel, 'we'll not argue the subject now: but I have a fancy to try my hand at rearing a young one; so intimate to your master that I must supply the place of this with my own, if he attempt to remove it. I don't engage to let Hareton go undisputed; but I'll be pretty sure to make the other come! Remember to tell him.'

This hint was enough to bind our hands. I repeated its substance on my return; and Edgar Linton, little interested at the commencement, spoke no more of interfering. I'm not aware that he could have done it to any purpose, had he been ever so willing.

The guest was now the master of Wuthering Heights: he held firm possession, and proved to the attorney—who, in his turn, proved it to Mr. Linton—that Earnshaw had mortgaged every yard of land he owned for cash to supply his mania for gaming; and he, Heathcliff, was the mortgagee. In that manner Hareton, who should now be the first gentleman in the neighbourhood, was reduced to a state of complete dependence on his father's inveterate enemy; and lives in his own house as a servant, deprived of the advantage of wages: quite unable to right himself, because of his friendlessness, and his ignorance that he has been wronged.

Analysis: Here we see the one of many reversals in the book. The son of Hindley, the former master, is now the servant. Ironically, he is much happier than his father ever was. It appears that his condition as a servant is a happy one because he is ignorant.

Discussion point: What you think of Heathcliff's treatment of Hareton?

Questions

Where does Isabella return to after the funeral?
What do we learn from Isabella happened after the funeral when Heathcliff returned?
How and why did Heathcliff hurt Isabella?
How did Isabella escape?
Where does Isabella go and what happens to her?
What happens six months after Catherine's death?
What does Edgar try to do with Hareton?
How does Heathcliff thwart Edgar's plans?
How does Heathcliff come to own Wuthering Heights?
Who lives there as a servant?
How does the author use the pathetic fallacy in this chapter?
GCSE style question: how and why is Heathcliff represented as brutal in this chapter?
GCSE style question: how does Brontë develop the theme of revenge in this chapter?
A Level style question: compare and contrast Brontë's presentation of revenge with another relevant text.
Creative response: write a poem/story called 'Revenge'.
Please find brief answers in section: **answers to questions**.

CHAPTER 18

Extract

The twelve years, continued Mrs. Dean, following that dismal period were the happiest of my life: my greatest troubles in their passage rose from our little lady's trifling illnesses, which she had to experience in common with all children, rich and poor. For the rest, after the first six months, she grew like a larch, and could walk and talk too, in her own way, before the heath blossomed a second time over Mrs. Linton's dust.

Analysis: Nelly is a surrogate mother to the young Cathy, but does not tell us much about her life with Cathy. The narrative barely exists when Heathcliff is not involved.

Discussion point: Why does Brontë present the new Cathy as much stronger and robust than her mother?

Extract

The abrupt descent of Penistone Crags particularly attracted her notice; especially when the setting sun shone on it and the topmost heights, and the whole extent of landscape besides lay in shadow. I explained that they were bare masses of stone, with hardly enough earth in their clefts to nourish a stunted tree.

'And why are they bright so long after it is evening here?' she pursued.

'Because they are a great deal higher up than we are,' replied I; 'you could not climb them, they are too high and steep. In winter the frost is always there before it comes to us; and deep into summer I have found snow under that black hollow on the north-east side!'

Analysis: Cathy's curiosity is one of her defining features. One of the pleasures of having a narrative that spans two generations is that it means that we, the reader, are aware of the previous generation's tragedies and problems, but certain characters, like Cathy and Hareton, are not. Thus Brontë creates a real sense of dramatic irony.

Discussion point Why does Brontë create so much dramatic irony in the second half of the novel?

Extract

This, however, is not making progress with my story. Miss Cathy rejected the peace-offering of the terrier, and demanded her own dogs, Charlie and Phoenix. They came limping and hanging their heads; and we set out for home, sadly out of sorts, every one of us. I could not wring from my little lady how she had spent the day; except that, as I supposed, the goal of her pilgrimage was Penistone Crags; and she arrived without adventure to the gate of the farm-house, when Hareton happened to issue forth, attended by some canine followers, who attacked her train. They had a smart battle, before their owners could separate them: that formed an introduction. Catherine told Hareton who she was, and where she was going; and asked him to show her the way: finally, beguiling him to accompany her. He opened the mysteries of the Fairy Cave, and twenty other queer places. But, being in disgrace, I was not favoured with a description of the interesting objects she saw. I could gather, however, that her guide had been a favourite till she hurt his feelings by addressing him as a servant; and Heathcliff's housekeeper hurt hers by calling him her cousin.

Analysis: Here we see that Hareton does not actually perceive himself as a servant, although his ill-educated talk, his lack of manners, marks him out as such. There is a sharp contrast between him and Cathy, who has clearly been brought up to be a lady. Thus we see a mirroring of the relationship between Heathcliff and his Cathy, her mother.

Discussion point: What are the similarities and differences between the relationship between Hareton and Cathy, and Heathcliff and the first Cathy?

Questions

What year/month does this chapter start in and how many years later is it?

How is Catherine junior similar and different to her mother?

Why does Edgar visit Isabella?

What does Cathy do?

Where does Nelly find her?

What does Nelly find out has happened?

What does Cathy mistake Hareton for?

How does she feel when learns Hareton is her cousin?

What does Nelly persuade Cathy not to do?

GCSE style question: what do you think of the presentation of Cathy in this chapter?

A Level style questions: compare and contrast Brontë's presentation of Catherine/Cathy with another mother/daughter in another text of your choice.

Creative response: write a poem/story called 'Mother and Daughter' or 'Father and Son'.

Please find brief answers in section: **answers to questions**.

CHAPTER 19

Extract

'This is your cousin Cathy, Linton,' he said, putting their little hands together. 'She's fond of you already; and mind you don't grieve her by crying to-night. Try to be cheerful now; the travelling is at an end, and you have nothing to do but rest and amuse yourself as you please.'

'Let me go to bed, then,' answered the boy, shrinking from Catherine's salute; and he put his fingers to remove incipient tears.

'Come, come, there's a good child,' I whispered, leading him in. 'You'll make her weep too—see how sorry she is for you!'

I do not know whether it was sorrow for him, but his cousin put on as sad a countenance as himself, and returned to her father. All three entered, and mounted to the library, where tea was laid ready. I proceeded to remove Linton's cap and mantle, and placed him on a chair by the table; but he was no sooner seated than he began to cry afresh. My master inquired what was the matter.

'I can't sit on a chair,' sobbed the boy.

'Go to the sofa, then, and Ellen shall bring you some tea,' answered his uncle patiently.

He had been greatly tried, during the journey, I felt convinced, by his fretful ailing charge. Linton slowly trailed himself off, and lay down. Cathy carried a footstool and her cup to his side.

> Analysis: Brontë's presentation of the young Linton is very acute: we have the very picture of a spoilt brat.

> Discussion point:_Why does Brontë make Linton such an unsympathetic character?

Questions

Who does Edgar bring back from London? What is he like?

How does Cathy treat the new arrival?

What does Joseph arrive and say? What is Edgar's response?

How is Linton similar and different to Heathcliff?

GCSE style question: what do you think of Brontë's representation of the second generation so far (Hareton, Cathy, Linton)?

A Level style question: compare and contrast Brontë's presentation of the second generation with another text which explores second generations.

Creative response: write a poem/story called 'My Inheritance' in which you explore what you have 'inherited' (in terms of personality/character etc.) from the people older than you.

Please find brief answers in section: **answers to questions**.

CHAPTER 20

Extract

'Don't mention his mother to me,' said the master, angrily. 'Get him something that he can eat, that's all. What is his usual food, Nelly?'

I suggested boiled milk or tea; and the housekeeper received instructions to prepare some. Come, I reflected, his father's selfishness may contribute to his comfort. He perceives his delicate constitution, and the necessity of treating him tolerably. I'll console Mr. Edgar by acquainting him with the turn Heathcliff's humour has taken. Having no excuse for lingering longer, I slipped out, while Linton was engaged in timidly rebuffing the advances of a friendly sheep-dog. But he was too much on the alert to be cheated: as I closed the door, I heard a cry, and a frantic repetition of the words—

'Don't leave me! I'll not stay here! I'll not stay here!'

Then the latch was raised and fell: they did not suffer him to come forth. I mounted Minny, and urged her to a trot; and so my brief guardianship ended.

Analysis: The leaving of Linton with Heathcliff is a poignant moment; we realise that this is the very worst thing that could happen to him.

Discussion point: Why does Heathcliff insist upon looking after Linton?

Questions

How does Nelly manage to get Linton to go to Heathcliff?
How does Heathcliff refer to Linton and Linton's mother when Linton arrives?
Why does Heathcliff like the fact that Linton is here?
What does Linton do as Nelly leaves?
GCSE style question: how does Brontë represent Heathcliff and his son in this chapter?
A Level style question: compare and contrast Brontë's presentation of 'villains' with another author who presents us with 'villains'.
Creative response: write a poem called 'I Hated Him'.
Please find brief answers in section: **answers to questions**.

CHAPTER 21

Extract

'Now, who is that?' asked Mr. Heathcliff, turning to Cathy. 'Can you tell?'
'Your son?' she said, having doubtfully surveyed, first one and then the other.
'Yes, yes,' answered he: 'but is this the only time you have beheld him? Think! Ah! you have a short memory. Linton, don't you recall your cousin, that you used to tease us so with wishing to see?'
'What, Linton!' cried Cathy, kindling into joyful surprise at the name. 'Is that little Linton! He's taller than I am! Are you Linton?'
The youth stepped forward, and acknowledged himself: she kissed him fervently, and they gazed with wonder at the change time had wrought in the appearance of each.

Analysis: Here we see the contrast between the impetuous, sensual Cathy and the limp, 'pretty' Linton who insists upon dry shoes.

Discussion point: Why is Cathy so drawn to Linton?

Extract

Linton gathered his energies, and left the hearth. The lattice was open, and, as he stepped out, I heard Cathy inquiring of her unsociable attendant what was that inscription over the door? Hareton stared up, and scratched his head like a true clown.

'It's some damnable writing,' he answered. 'I cannot read it.'

'Can't read it?' cried Catherine; 'I can read it: it's English. But I want to know why it is there.'

Linton giggled: the first appearance of mirth he had exhibited.

'He does not know his letters,' he said to his cousin. 'Could you believe in the existence of such a colossal dunce?'

'Is he all as he should be?' asked Miss Cathy, seriously; 'or is he simple: not right? I've questioned him twice now, and each time he looked so stupid I think he does not understand me. I can hardly understand him, I'm sure!'

Linton repeated his laugh, and glanced at Hareton tauntingly; who certainly did not seem quite clear of comprehension at that moment.

'There's nothing the matter but laziness; is there, Earnshaw?' he said. 'My cousin fancies you are an idiot. There you experience the consequence of scorning "book-larning," as you would say. Have you noticed, Catherine, his frightful Yorkshire pronunciation?'

'Why, where the devil is the use on't?' growled Hareton, more ready in answering his daily companion. He was about to enlarge further, but the two youngsters broke into a noisy fit of merriment: my giddy miss being delighted to discover that she might turn his strange talk to matter of amusement.

Analysis: Here we see the younger generation interacting with each other. Linton's sniggering at Hareton's illiteracy creates a real sense of tension and sympathy for Hareton.

Discussion point: Why does Brontë make Hareton such a sympathetic character at this point?

Extract

'I will have one, you cruel wretch!' she screamed, darting her hand into the fire, and drawing forth some half-consumed fragments, at the expense of her fingers.

'Very well—and I will have some to exhibit to papa!' I answered, shaking back the rest into the bundle, and turning anew to the door.

She emptied her blackened pieces into the flames, and motioned me to finish the immolation. It was done; I stirred up the ashes, and interred them under a shovelful of coals; and she mutely, and with a sense of intense injury, retired to her private apartment. I descended to tell my master that the young lady's qualm of sickness was almost gone, but I judged it best for her to lie down a while. She wouldn't dine; but she reappeared at tea, pale, and red about the eyes, and marvellously subdued in outward aspect. Next morning I answered the letter by a slip of paper, inscribed, 'Master Heathcliff is requested to send no more notes to Miss Linton, as she will not receive them.' And, henceforth, the little boy came with vacant pockets.

Analysis: The conflicts of the previous generation are visited upon the new one: Edgar refuses to countenance his daughter seeing the son of Heathcliff. As a result, a secret correspondence occurs between Cathy and Linton, which Ellen finds out about and puts a stop to, threatening to tell Edgar.

Discussion point: How does Brontë explore the themes of censorship and secrecy here?

Questions

What does Cathy persuade Nelly to do on the anniversary of her mother's death?

Who do they meet there?

What plan do we learn Heathcliff has? What happens when Cathy meets Linton and Hareton?

What does Heathcliff confess about Hareton?

How does Cathy bond with Linton?

How does Brontë build suspense in this chapter?

What echoes are there in Linton's mocking of Hareton?

How is Linton's mockery of Hareton different from Edgar's mockery of Heathcliff?

GCSE style question: how does Brontë present the theme of mockery in this chapter?

A Level style question: compare and contrast Brontë's exploration of mockery with another relevant text.

Creative response: write a poem/story called 'They Mocked Me'.

Please find brief answers in section: **answers to questions**.

CHAPTER 22

Extract

Summer drew to an end, and early autumn: it was past Michaelmas, but the harvest was late that year, and a few of our fields were still uncleared. Mr. Linton and his daughter would frequently walk out among the reapers; at the carrying of the last sheaves they stayed till dusk, and the evening happening to be chill and damp, my master caught a bad cold, that settled obstinately on his lungs, and confined him indoors throughout the whole of the winter, nearly without intermission.

Poor Cathy, frightened from her little romance, had been considerably sadder and duller since its abandonment; and her father insisted on her reading less, and taking more exercise.

Analysis: We see how Cathy is affected by the end of the romance; Wuthering Heights for her represents something entirely different from the other characters.

Discussion point: What does Wuthering Heights represent for Cathy?

Questions

Why does Cathy not think of Linton much during the winter?

What does the loss of Cathy's hat lead to?

What does he tell Cathy off for?

What does he say about Linton? Why does Cathy go to Wuthering Heights?

How does Nelly's treatment of Cathy differ from her treatment of Catherine, her mother?

GCSE style question: how does Brontë present both Catherine and Cathy in the novel?

A Level style question: compare and contrast Brontë's presentation of Nelly with another similar figure (e.g. governess/teacher/nanny/care-giver) in another relevant text.

Creative response: write a poem/story called 'I Had To Tell Him'.

Please find brief answers in section: **answers to questions**.

CHAPTER 23

Extract

Cathy began searching for some water; she lighted on a pitcher in the dresser, filled a tumbler, and brought it. He bid her add a spoonful of wine from a bottle on the table; and having swallowed a small portion, appeared more tranquil, and said she was very kind.

'And are you glad to see me?' asked she, reiterating her former question and pleased to detect the faint dawn of a smile.

'Yes, I am. It's something new to hear a voice like yours!' he replied. 'But I have been vexed, because you wouldn't come. And papa swore it was owing to me: he called me a pitiful, shuffling, worthless thing; and said you despised me; and if he had been in my place, he would be more the master of the Grange than your father by this time. But you don't despise me, do you, Miss—?'

Analysis: Heathcliff lures Cathy back to Wuthering Heights saying that Linton is dying of a broken heart. Cathy now learns that this is a ruse. The plot becomes a Gothic melodrama with Heathcliff playing the role of scheming villain.

Discussion point: What is revealed about Linton here? What do you think of his characterisation?

Questions

What is the weather like as Cathy and Nelly travel to Wuthering Heights? Why does Cathy feel conflicted?

What does Linton complain about when they get there?

How does Cathy respond when Linton talks about love?

How does Linton deepen Cathy's guilty feelings?

How does Cathy try to solve things? GCSE style question: how does Brontë explore the theme of guilt in chapters 22 and 23? A Level style question: compare and contrast Brontë's exploration of the theme of guilt with another relevant text.

Creative response: write a poem called 'Guilt'.

Please find brief answers in section: **answers to questions**.

CHAPTER 24

Questions

What does Cathy confess to Nelly?

Why does Hareton become angry and what does he do as a result?

Who does Linton blame for incident and why is he so upset? How does Hareton try to apologise and why does his apology fail?

What does Cathy learn to do with Linton later on in the chapter?

What does Edgar do when he learns of Cathy's visits to the Heights?

What does Nelly not tell Edgar and what is the result?

GCSE style question: how does Brontë develop Hareton's character in this chapter?

GCSE style question: how do we see Nelly developing as a character in this chapter?

A Level style question: compare and contrast Brontë's presentation of Hareton with a similar character in another text.

Creative response: write a poem/story called 'Uneducated'.

Please find brief answers in section: **answers to questions**.

CHAPTER 25

Questions

Why does Nelly continue with her story?
What does Nelly Edgar about Linton?
What does Edgar eventually concede?
Where does Edgar agree Cathy can meet Linton and what condition?
GCSE style question: how is Edgar presented in this chapter and the rest of the book?
A Level style question: compare and contrast the presentation of Edgar with another similar figure in another relevant text.
Creative response: write a poem/story called 'The Misguided Parent'.
Please find brief answers in section: **answers to questions**.

CHAPTER 26

Questions

Why is Linton not at the agreed place?
Why is Linton's health an issue?
What is Linton's mood?
What does Linton extract from Cathy?
What do Cathy and Nelly discuss?
GCSE style question: how is Linton presented differently in this chapter?
A Level style question: compare and contrast the representation of Linton with a similar figure in another relevant text.
Creative response: write a poem called 'I Felt Sorry for Him/Her'.
Please find brief answers in section: **answers to questions**.

CHAPTER 27

Extract

Regardless of this warning, she captured his closed hand and its contents again. 'We will go!' she repeated, exerting her utmost efforts to cause the iron muscles to relax; and finding that her nails made no impression, she applied her teeth pretty sharply. Heathcliff glanced at me a glance that kept me from interfering a moment. Catherine was too intent on his fingers to notice his face. He opened them suddenly, and resigned the object of dispute; but, ere she had well secured it, he seized her with the liberated hand, and, pulling her on his knee, administered with the other a shower of terrific slaps on both sides of the head, each sufficient to have fulfilled his threat, had she been able to fall.

At this diabolical violence I rushed on him furiously. 'You villain!' I began to cry, 'you villain!' A touch on the chest silenced me: I am stout, and soon put out of breath; and, what with that and the rage, I staggered dizzily back and felt ready to suffocate, or to burst a blood-vessel. The scene was over in two minutes; Catherine, released, put her two hands to her temples, and looked just as if she were not sure whether her ears were off or on. She trembled like a reed, poor thing, and leant against the table perfectly bewildered.

'I know how to chastise children, you see,' said the scoundrel, grimly, as he stooped to repossess himself of the key, which had dropped to the floor. 'Go to Linton now, as I told you; and cry at your ease! I shall be your father, to-morrow—all the father you'll have in a few days—and you shall have plenty of that. You can bear plenty; you're no weakling: you shall have a daily taste, if I catch such a devil of a temper in your eyes again!'

Cathy ran to me instead of Linton, and knelt down and put her burning cheek on my lap, weeping aloud.

Analysis: Here we see Heathcliff presented a genuine villain, entrapping Cathy into his diabolical plan of revenge. Cathy is spirited in her rebellion against him, but her efforts are ineffectual.

Discussion point:_How and why does Brontë present Heathcliff as a villain here?

Extract

'Stay all night? No,' she said, looking slowly round. 'Ellen, I'll burn that door down but I'll get out.'

And she would have commenced the execution of her threat directly, but Linton was up in alarm for his dear self again. He clasped her in his two feeble arms sobbing:—'Won't you have me, and save me? not let me come to the Grange? Oh, darling Catherine! you mustn't go and leave, after all. You must obey my father—you must!'

'I must obey my own,' she replied, 'and relieve him from this cruel suspense. The whole night! What would he think? He'll be distressed already. I'll either break or burn a way out of the house. Be quiet! You're in no danger; but if you hinder me—Linton, I love papa better than you!' The mortal terror he felt of Mr. Heathcliff's anger restored to the boy his coward's eloquence. Catherine was near distraught: still, she persisted that she must go home, and tried entreaty in her turn, persuading him to subdue his selfish agony. While they were thus occupied, our jailor re-entered.

Analysis: Here we find Cathy trapped by many things: physically jailed by Heathcliff, concerned for Linton and terrified of the effect her disappearance will have upon her sick father. Ellen is imprisoned by Hareton, who won't speak to his former surrogate mother and only gives her basic food. Fortunately, Ellen is able to return home to

Thrushcross Grange to tend to the dying Edgar. Cathy marries Linton, but escapes with the help of Linton just in time to say goodbye to her father before he dies; in such a way, Heathcliff plan of revenge fails in part because Edgar dies a happy man, knowing his daughter is well and loves him.

Discussion point: How and why does Brontë put such importance upon the moments of dying in this novel?

Questions

Who is dying?

Why does Cathy go with Nelly and meet Linton?

What is Linton terrified about?

Who appears and what does he persuade Cathy and Nelly to do?

What happens to Nelly and Cathy at the Heights?

What does Linton tell them when Heathcliff goes for horses?

On what condition does Cathy say she will marry Linton?

What is Heathcliff's response?

GCSE style question: how does Brontë suggest that Cathy is like her mother in this chapter?

GCSE style question: how does Brontë suggest Linton's selfishness?

A Level style question: compare and contrast Brontë's exploration of male violence with another similar text.

Creative response: write a poem called 'He Hit Me'.

Please find brief answers in section: **answers to questions**.

CHAPTER 28

Questions

Who releases Nelly and when?

What does Linton tell Nelly?

How does Heathcliff manage to stop Edgar making sure Linton won't get Cathy's property?

How does Cathy manage to comfort her father before he dies?

Who does Edgar feel convinced he will join in death?

Who is now in control?

GCSE style question: how does Brontë explore the theme of violence in this chapter?

A Level style question: compare and contrast Brontë's exploration of patriarchy with another text where it is a relevant issue.

Creative response: write a poem/story called 'It's A Man's World'.

Please find brief answers in section: **answers to questions**.

CHAPTER 29

Questions

Why has Heathcliff punished Linton?
Why does Heathcliff refuse to let Cathy live at the Grange?
Why does Cathy have to obey Heathcliff and Linton?
How does Cathy stand up to Heathcliff?
What does Heathcliff confess to Nelly as Cathy packs her things?
What does Heathcliff instruct Nelly not to do?
GCSE style question: how does Brontë make Heathcliff a complex character in this chapter and at other parts in the novel?
A Level style question: compare and contrast Brontë's presentation of Heathcliff with a similarly Romantic figure in another significant text.
Creative response: write a poem/story called 'Ghosts'.
Please find brief answers in section: **answers to questions**.

CHAPTER 30

Extract

Thus ended Mrs. Dean's story. Notwithstanding the doctor's prophecy, I am rapidly recovering strength; and though it be only the second week in January, I propose getting out on horseback in a day or two, and riding over to Wuthering Heights, to inform my landlord that I shall spend the next six months in London; and, if he likes, he may look out for another tenant to take the place after October. I would not pass another winter here for much.

Analysis: Here we learn that Heathcliff now has all the property, now that his son has died. His revenge against her family is complete; he now has everything. From being the homeless, penniless servant to Hindley, he owns all the property with the daughter of his most bitter enemy at his mercy.

Discussion point: How does Brontë create a sense of a real cycle of events happening here? Why is Heathcliff so obsessed with claiming the property?

Questions

Who now gives us information about Cathy? Why do Zillah and Hareton not help Cathy?
Who looks exclusively after Linton until he dies? How does Cathy behave after his death and why?
What does Lockwood tell Nelly?

What evidence is there that there is an attraction between Hareton and Cathy? Why does Heathcliff want to stop any romance between Hareton and Cathy?

GCSE style question: how does this chapter make the story come full circle?

A Level style question: compare and contrast Brontë's narrative structure with another story which 'comes full circle'.

Creative response: write a poem/story called 'Full Circle'.

Please find brief answers in section: **answers to questions**.

CHAPTER 31

Questions

Why can't Cathy respond to Nelly's letter?

How does Cathy humiliate Hareton?

How does Hareton respond?

What does Lockwood overhear Heathcliff saying about Hareton?

What does Lockwood realise as he rides back to the Grange?

How do we see Heathcliff changing in this chapter?

GCSE style question: what do you think of Brontë's presentation of Cathy and Hareton?

A Level style question: compare and contrast Brontë's presentation of cousins with another text which explores the issue.

Creative response: write a poem called 'Cousins'.

Please find brief answers in section: **answers to questions**.

CHAPTER 32

Extract

1802.—This September I was invited to devastate the moors of a friend in the north, and on my journey to his abode, I unexpectedly came within fifteen miles of Gimmerton. The ostler at a roadside public-house was holding a pail of water to refresh my horses, when a cart of very green oats, newly reaped, passed by, and he remarked,—'Yon's frough Gimmerton, nah! They're allas three wick' after other folk wi' ther harvest.'

'Gimmerton?' I repeated—my residence in that locality had already grown dim and dreamy. 'Ah! I know. How far is it from this?'

'Happen fourteen mile o'er th' hills; and a rough road,' he answered.

A sudden impulse seized me to visit Thrushcross Grange.

Analysis: Lockwood, like the reader, is intoxicated by the narrative and by Cathy, drawn back to the mystery of the moors and the story.

Discussion point: What do we think of Lockwood at this point in the novel? How have our feelings towards him changed?

Extract

'He's just like a dog, is he not, Ellen?' she once observed, 'or a cart-horse? He does his work, eats his food, and sleeps eternally! What a blank, dreary mind he must have! Do you ever dream, Hareton? And, if you do, what is it about? But you can't speak to me!'

Then she looked at him; but he would neither open his mouth nor look again.

'He's, perhaps, dreaming now,' she continued. 'He twitched his shoulder as Juno twitches hers. Ask him, Ellen.'

'Mr. Hareton will ask the master to send you up-stairs, if you don't behave!' I said. He had not only twitched his shoulder but clenched his fist, as if tempted to use it.

'I know why Hareton never speaks, when I am in the kitchen,' she exclaimed, on another occasion. 'He is afraid I shall laugh at him. Ellen, what do you think? He began to teach himself to read once; and, because I laughed, he burned his books, and dropped it: was he not a fool?'

Analysis: Here we see the development of the relationship between Cathy and Hareton. It is interesting to speculate upon Brontë's purposes here: she almost seems to be suggesting that Cathy and Hareton are breaking the cycle of abuse that has occurred over the generations because Hareton is willing to accept a subservient role to a powerful woman.

Discussion point: At this point in the novel, it might be fruitful to compare Hareton and Cathy to other characters in the book. In what ways is Hareton similar and different to: Hindley, Heathcliff and Edgar Linton? In what ways is Cathy similar and different to her mother?

Extract

'I didn't know you took my part,' she answered, drying her eyes; 'and I was miserable and bitter at everybody; but now I thank you, and beg you to forgive me: what can I do besides?'

She returned to the hearth, and frankly extended her hand. He blackened and scowled like a thunder-cloud, and kept his fists resolutely clenched, and his gaze fixed on the ground. Catherine, by instinct, must have divined it was obdurate perversity, and not dislike, that prompted this dogged conduct; for, after remaining an instant undecided, she stooped and impressed on his cheek a gentle kiss. The little rogue thought I had not seen her, and, drawing back, she took her former station by the window, quite demurely. I shook my head reprovingly, and then she blushed and whispered—'Well! what should I have done, Ellen? He wouldn't shake hands, and he wouldn't look: I must show him some way that I like him—that I want to be friends.'

Analysis: Cathy's growing interest in Hareton is fascinating; she is now losing her social snobbery. She realises that Hareton is not to blame for his lack of education.

Discussion point: _Why is education such an important theme in the novel?

Extract

'Tak' these in to t' maister, lad,' he said, 'and bide there. I's gang up to my own rahm. This hoile's neither mensful nor seemly for us: we mun side out and seearch another.'

'Come, Catherine,' I said, 'we must "side out" too: I've done my ironing. Are you ready to go?'

'It is not eight o'clock!' she answered, rising unwillingly.

'Hareton, I'll leave this book upon the chimney-piece, and I'll bring some more to-morrow.'

'Ony books that yah leave, I shall tak' into th' hahse,' said Joseph, 'and it'll be mitch if yah find 'em agean; soa, yah may plase yerseln!'

Cathy threatened that his library should pay for hers; and, smiling as she passed Hareton, went singing up-stairs: lighter of heart, I venture to say, than ever she had been under that roof before; except, perhaps, during her earliest visits to Linton.

The intimacy thus commenced grew rapidly; though it encountered temporary interruptions. Earnshaw was not to be civilized with a wish, and my young lady was no philosopher, and no paragon of patience; but both their minds tending to the same point—one loving and desiring to esteem, and the other loving and desiring to be esteemed—they contrived in the end to reach it.

You see, Mr. Lockwood, it was easy enough to win Mrs. Heathcliff's heart. But now, I'm glad you did not try. The crown of all my wishes will be the union of those two. I shall envy no one on their wedding day: there won't be a happier woman than myself in England!

Analysis: Nelly obviously wants the two children who she brought up to fall in love. This is clearly not something Lockwood particularly wants, having, in part, returned to Wuthering Heights hoping to propose to Catherine.

Discussion point: What do you think of Hareton and Cathy's romance?

Questions

When does Lockwood visit the Grange again? How much time has passed since he was at the Grange?

Where has Nelly moved to? How are things different? How is Cathy helping Hareton?

Why does Lockwood feel envious? Why is Joseph disgusted?

What news does Nelly give Lockwood?

How is the story between Hareton and Cathy similar to Beauty and the Beast?

How have books brought Hareton and Cathy together?

GCSE style question: how does Brontë present the relationship of Hareton and Cathy in the novel?

A Level style question: compare and contrast Brontë's presentation of time with another text which explores this issue.

Creative response: write Hareton's diary for this chapter and other parts of the novel.

Please find brief answers in section: **answers to questions**.

CHAPTER 33

Extract

The latter was speechless; his cousin replied—'You shouldn't grudge a few yards of earth for me to ornament, when you have taken all my land!'

'Your land, insolent slut! You never had any,' said Heathcliff.

'And my money,' she continued; returning his angry glare, and meantime biting a piece of crust, the remnant of her breakfast.

'Silence!' he exclaimed. 'Get done, and begone!'

'And Hareton's land, and his money,' pursued the reckless thing. 'Hareton and I are friends now; and I shall tell him all about you!'

The master seemed confounded a moment: he grew pale, and rose up, eyeing her all the while, with an expression of mortal hate.

'If you strike me, Hareton will strike you,' she said; 'so you may as well sit down.'

'If Hareton does not turn you out of the room, I'll strike him to hell,' thundered Heathcliff. 'Damnable witch! dare you pretend to rouse him against me? Off with her! Do you hear? Fling her into the kitchen! I'll kill her, Ellen Dean, if you let her come into my sight again!'

Analysis: Brontë presents us with some complex alliances and conflicts here. Hareton is obviously devoted to Heathcliff and Cathy but himself in the middle of both of these two powerful characters' argument. It is clear that Heathcliff has trained Hareton to be obedient like a dog.

Discussion point: How does Brontë create suspense in this scene?

Extract

The two new friends established themselves in the house during his absence; where I heard Hareton sternly check his cousin, on her offering a revelation of her father-in-law's conduct to his father. He said he wouldn't suffer a word to be uttered in his disparagement: if he were the devil, it didn't signify; he would stand by him; and he'd rather she would abuse himself, as she used to, than begin on Mr. Heathcliff. Catherine was waxing cross at this; but he found means to make her hold her tongue, by asking how she would like him to speak ill of her father? Then she comprehended that Earnshaw took the master's reputation home to himself; and was attached by ties stronger than reason could break— chains, forged by habit, which it would be cruel to attempt to loosen. She showed a good heart, thenceforth, in avoiding both complaints and expressions of antipathy concerning Heathcliff; and confessed to me her sorrow that she had endeavoured to raise a bad spirit between him and Hareton: indeed, I don't believe she has ever breathed a syllable, in the latter's hearing, against her oppressor since.

Analysis: Hareton's devotion to Heathcliff, his master, is touching; we realise that Heathcliff has treated Hareton much better than Hindley ever treated him. Cathy too begins to appreciate Heathcliff more.

Discussion point: Why is Hareton so loyal to Heathcliff? Are there things that have happened that Nelly has not informed us of? If so, why does Brontë only present us with Nelly's side of the story?

Extract

'Nelly, there is a strange change approaching; I'm in its shadow at present. I take so little interest in my daily life that I hardly remember to eat and drink. Those two who have left the room are the only objects which retain a distinct material appearance to me; and that appearance causes me pain, amounting to agony. About her I won't speak; and I don't desire to think; but I earnestly wish she were invisible: her presence invokes only maddening sensations. He moves me differently: and yet if I could do it without seeming insane, I'd never see him again! You'll perhaps think me rather inclined to become so,' he added, making an effort to smile, 'if I try to describe the thousand forms of past associations and ideas he awakens or embodies. But you'll not talk of what I tell you; and my mind is so eternally secluded in itself, it is tempting at last to turn it out to another.

'Five minutes ago Hareton seemed a personification of my youth, not a human being; I felt to him in such a variety of ways, that it would have been impossible to have accosted him rationally. In the first place, his startling likeness to Catherine connected him fearfully with her. That, however, which you may suppose the most potent to arrest my imagination, is actually the least: for what is not connected with her to me? and what does not recall her? I cannot look down to this floor, but her features are shaped in the flags! In every cloud, in every tree—filling the air at night, and caught by glimpses in every object by day—I am surrounded with her image! The most ordinary faces of men and women—my own features—mock me with a resemblance. The entire world is a dreadful collection of memoranda that she did exist, and that I have lost her!

> Analysis: Towards the end of the novel, the theme of the supernatural returns. We have already seen how Heathcliff has disinterred Cathy's body in order to see her again after the death of Edgar Linton: he has been yearning to be unified with her again. But this is not enough; ultimately he needs a spiritual union with her, which can only be found in death.

> Discussion point: What are feelings towards Heathcliff at this point in the novel? How does Brontë try to create real feelings of pathos here?

Questions

What do Hareton and Cathy do to Joseph's blackcurrant bushes?

What is Cathy's response when Joseph complains?

What does Heathcliff do when he learns that she has said this?

What does Heathcliff feel Cathy's face looks like? What does he tell Cathy about his desire for revenge?

What does he confess?

What does he become obsessed by?

GCSE style question: how does Brontë present Heathcliff in this chapter?

A Level style question: compare and contrast Brontë's presentation of loneliness with another text which explores the issue.

Creative response: write a poem/story called 'Lonely'.

Please find brief answers in section: **answers to questions**.

CHAPTER 34

Extract

'Yes, close it,' he replied, in his familiar voice. 'There, that is pure awkwardness! Why did you hold the candle horizontally? Be quick, and bring another.'

I hurried out in a foolish state of dread, and said to Joseph—'The master wishes you to take him a light and rekindle the fire.' For I dared not go in myself again just then.

Joseph rattled some fire into the shovel, and went: but he brought it back immediately, with the supper-tray in his other hand, explaining that Mr. Heathcliff was going to bed, and he wanted nothing to eat till morning. We heard him mount the stairs directly; he did not proceed to his ordinary chamber, but turned into that with the panelled bed: its window, as I mentioned before, is wide enough for anybody to get through; and it struck me that he plotted another midnight excursion, of which he had rather we had no suspicion.

Analysis: Once again, Brontë emphasises the blissful nature of death; it is clear that Heathcliff feels he is going to heaven. It is perhaps not surprising that Sylvia Plath, one of the most famous poets of the twentieth century, was enraptured and entranced by *Wuthering Heights*, writing about it in a poem: Emily's promotion of death as a beautiful and divine thing makes Emily one of the first writers who really celebrated suicide. Plath's cultish appreciation of Emily Brontë is perhaps one of the factors that led her to commit suicide.

Discussion point: Why do you think Heathcliff thinks he is going to heaven?

Extract

'When day breaks I'll send for Green,' he said; 'I wish to make some legal inquiries of him while I can bestow a thought on those matters, and while I can act calmly. I have not written my will yet; and how to leave my property I cannot determine. I wish I could annihilate it from the face of the earth.'

'I would not talk so, Mr. Heathcliff,' I interposed. 'Let your will be a while: you'll be spared to repent of your many injustices yet! I never expected that your nerves would be disordered: they are, at present, marvellously so, however; and almost entirely through your own fault. The way you've passed these three last days might knock up a Titan. Do take some food, and some repose. You need only look at yourself in a glass to see how you require both. Your cheeks are hollow, and your eyes blood-shot, like a person starving with hunger and going blind with loss of sleep.'

'It is not my fault that I cannot eat or rest,' he replied. 'I assure you it is through no settled designs. I'll do both, as soon as I possibly can. But you might as well bid a man struggling in the water rest within arms' length of the shore! I must reach it first, and then I'll rest.

Analysis: Here we see Heathcliff thinking about the practicalities of death quite coldly. We also see that Nelly is upset by the prospect of him dying. Her shifting feelings towards him mirror the reader's in changing feelings: while we may not agree with all her judgements upon him, we have had moments when we have condemned him as strongly as she does, and moments when we have felt sorry for him – as she does here.

Discussion point: Why is Nelly so upset? How do you feel towards Heathcliff at this point?

Extract

'Th' divil's harried off his soul,' he cried, 'and he may hev' his carcass into t' bargin, for aught I care! Ech! what a wicked 'un he looks, girning at death!' and the old sinner grinned in mockery. I thought he intended to cut a caper round the bed; but suddenly composing himself, he fell on his knees, and raised his hands, and returned thanks that the lawful master and the ancient stock were restored to their rights.

I felt stunned by the awful event; and my memory unavoidably recurred to former times with a sort of oppressive sadness. But poor Hareton, the most wronged, was the only one who really suffered much. He sat by the corpse all night, weeping in bitter earnest. He pressed its hand, and kissed the sarcastic, savage face that every one else shrank from contemplating; and bemoaned him with that strong grief which springs naturally from a generous heart, though it be tough as tempered steel.

Analysis: The final death scene in the novel is curiously placid. Heathcliff, who was so animated in life, is 'perfectly still'. It is a poignant scene: recently we have only seen him being an abuser, now we see him abusing himself and curiously feel sorry for him.

Discussion point: Why is Hareton so grief stricken? How successful is this death scene? What makes it rather eerie and poignant?

Extract

I sought, and soon discovered, the three headstones on the slope next the moor: the middle one grey, and half buried in the heath; Edgar Linton's only harmonized by the turf and moss creeping up its foot; Heathcliff's still bare.

I lingered round them, under that benign sky: watched the moths fluttering among the heath and harebells, listened to the soft wind breathing through the grass, and wondered how any one could ever imagine unquiet slumbers for the sleepers in that quiet earth.

Analysis: The famous last paragraph of the novel is wonderfully serene, suggesting that it is beyond the imagination of us to think that the dead in the ground are "unquiet". We are left with a sense that death has solved all the problems of the novel. In such a way,

Brontë suggests that death is a release, a running theme of all her work.

Discussion point: How successful is this resolution to the novel?

Questions

What do Hareton and Cathy do in the nice April weather?
What does Heathcliff do?
How does he die?
Where is he buried and who comes to the funeral?
What have the local people seen?
What does Lockwood see before he leaves the area and what does he imagine? Why is the ending possibly ironic?
GCSE style question: how does Brontë make the death of Heathcliff so compelling and poignant?
A Level style question: compare and contrast Brontë's death scenes with another text which describes people's deaths.
Creative response: write Cathy's diary for the novel.
Devise a **visual organizer** of the key events/characters/literary techniques in the novel; you should decide upon one of these things to focus upon depending upon what you feel you need to work upon the most.
Please find brief answers in section: **answers to questions**.

Answers to the questions

NOTE: the answers to these questions are deliberately very brief; many of them could be much longer, particularly the answers to the GCSE/ A Level/Creative Response questions which require argumentative, evaluative and personal responses as well as creative thought.

Chapter 1

What house is Mr Lockwood renting and why? Thrushcross Grange. He is recovering from an encounter with a girl he met that summer. He found her fascinating but when she expressed feelings for him, he ended the relationship.
What does 'wuthering' mean? Stormy.
What is the penetralium? The inner most part of the house.
How friendly are Heathcliff and Joseph? Unfriendly.
What condition is the property in at Wuthering Heights? Poor.

What interests Lockwood which is over the door and why? Carvings.

Why is Lockwood interested by Heathcliff? He thinks Heathcliff is similar to him, despite the fact that he doesn't speak much.

What happens when he is left in a room? He is attacked by dogs.

GCSE style question: how effective is this opening to the novel? What are its strengths and weaknesses? You could talk about how the novel has the classic trope of the "stranger who comes to town" (Lockwood) and encounters mysteries which intrigue him (the carvings/the setting) and hostility (Heathcliff).

Chapter 2

Who does Lockwood mistake the young, unfriendly girl for? He thinks she is Heathcliff's wife.

What does he later assume about the girl? That she is the young man's wife.

What does he think of the young man? He is thinks he is 'bordering on the repulsive' and is the husband of the girl.

What does he later learn about the girl and man? That her husband is dead, and that he is Hareton Earnshaw and not Heathcliff's son.

What happens to the weather after supper? It snows.

What does Lockwood do when no one will help him home? He grabs a lantern.

Why does he not get home? He is attacked by the dogs and the snow is impassable.

Who is the housekeeper and how does she help Lockwood? Zillah. She shows him to a room.

Why do we learn that Lockwood is an unreliable narrator in this chapter? Lockwood gets so many things wrong such as who is married to whom.

Why are all the doors and gates barred and chained? So that the girl can't leave the house.

What does 'whisht' mean? Be quiet.

GCSE style question: How does Brontë create a sense of menace and confusion in this chapter?

Chapter 3

What is special about the bed that Lockwood finds? It has sliding panels.

What names are scratched on the window sill? Catherine Earnshaw, Catherine Heathcliff, Catherine Linton.

What is the name inside the Bible? Catherine Linton.

What is scrawled in the margins of the books? A diary talking about Catherine and Heathcliff, about how they used to escape to the moors, and then how were punished for it.

What does Lockwood dream when he falls asleep? He is listening to a famous preacher, and then is attacked by the congregation.

Why does he wake? A branch is tapping at the window.

What happens in his second dream? He tries to stop the tapping by smashing the window; he is grabbed by a hand of someone who says they are Catherine Linton, asking to be let in.

How does he wake? He wakes shouting in horror.

What is Heathcliff's response when Lockwood tells him about his dream? He calls out for Catherine.

How does the author present dreams in this chapter?

What does 'flaysome' mean? Dreadful.

Who is 'owd Nick'? The Devil.

GCSE style question: how does Brontë create a sense of the supernatural in this chapter? The dreams, the tapping at the window, the talk about the Devil etc.

Chapter 4

Why does he ask Mrs Dean about the family at Wuthering Heights? He is curious.

What does she tell him? That Mrs Heathcliff is the daughter of the person who used to be her master, Mr Linton.

What do we learn about Heathcliff's childhood? He was brought to the Heights by her previous master, Mr Earnshaw.

Who resented Heathcliff, how old were they and what did they do to him? The master's two children, Hindley, 14, Catherine, 6, and the master's wife. They bullied him.

What happened to Heathcliff and Catherine? They became close friends.

Why did Nelly warm to Heathcliff? How he was so patient about being ill and being bullied by Hindley.

GCSE style question: how is Heathcliff presented in this chapter? Why do you think the author presents him as a victim?

Chapter 5

Who does Earnshaw like the most before he dies? Heathcliff becomes Earnshaw's favourite.

What does Hindley feel? He resents Heathcliff.

How does old Earnshaw treat Catherine and why? Very strictly, being influenced by Joseph's religious ideas.

How do Catherine and Heathcliff respond to old Earnshaw's death? They are grief-stricken.

What does Nelly do when she sees the children so upset? She runs through the storm and gets the doctor.

What does Nelly think of the children when she returns? That they seem very innocent thinking Mr Earnshaw is in heaven.

How does the author and Nelly, the narrator, present Catherine in this chapter? She has both charming and unlikeable characteristics.

GCSE style question: how is Heathcliff and Catherine's relationship presented in this chapter? They are very close.

Chapter 6

Who does Hindley return with after the funeral? A wife.

What job does Hindley give Heathcliff and how does he restrict him? A farm labourer. He stops him from being educated.

How do Catherine and Heathcliff escape from Hindley's bullying? By going to the moors.

What does Heathcliff tell Nelly one evening? That they have been to Thrushcross Grange and seen the Linton family through a window. Catherine was attacked by a dog and taken in. Heathcliff was deemed 'unfit' to come into the house. He would have smashed the window to rescue Cathy but saw she was happy.

How does Mr Linton tell off Hindley? That he shouldn't let Catherine be with Heathcliff because he is so coarse.

What is the effect of the different narrators in this chapter? Nelly and Heathcliff are striking contrasts: his passionate language compared with her more sedate style.

GCSE style question: how does the author build sympathy for Heathcliff? He is presented as both passionate, active, intelligent, but also a victim.

A Level style question: how are the places of Thrushcross Grange and Wuthering Heights similar and different in this chapter? Thrushcross Grange represents civilization, order and refinement while the Heights represents wildness, anarchy, passion.

Chapter 7

How long does Catherine stay at the Grange? How is she different when she returns? 5 weeks. She returns a finely dressed lady.

How has Heathcliff been treated? Like a servant.

Why is Heathcliff upset by Catherine? She laughs at his uncouthness.

How does Heathcliff make a big effort for Catherine? He dresses up as best he can.

What does Edgar say about Heathcliff's appearance? He makes fun of it.

What is Heathcliff's response and what does Hindley do? He throws hot sauce over Egdar and is beaten by Hindley.

What does Catherine do to help Heathcliff? She climbs into Heathcliff's room, where he has been locked up.

What does Heathcliff promise to do? To get revenge.

GCSE style question: how does the author present the themes of social justice and ambition in this chapter? Heathcliff is presented as being treated unfairly, the victim of social snobbery (Edgar) and brutal jealousy (Hindley).

A Level style question: compare and contrast the way in which this novel explores social justice with another text of your choice.

Chapter 8

What happens to Hindley's wife? She dies in child birth.

What is Hindley's response? He becomes a drunk, bullying Heathcliff even more.

What problem does Catherine have? She likes both Edgar Linton and Heathcliff, and is torn between the two.

What does Catherine criticise Heathcliff for? His lack of educated conversation.

How does the relationship between Edgar and Catherine develop? Catherine falls out with Heathcliff over Edgar's visit, she treats both Nelly and Edgar badly, but then when Edgar tries to leave, she stops him and they say they are lovers.

How does the author present Catherine in this chapter? She is presented as conflicted, difficult, changeable in mood and attitude.

GCSE style question: how is imagery used in this chapter? Animalistic imagery is connected with both Heathcliff and Edgar.

Chapter 9

How does Heathcliff save Hareton? He catches him when Hindley drops him over a banister.

What does Catherine tell Nelly? That she is going to marry Edgar. She knows this is wrong.

What dream does Catherine tell Nelly about? That she was thrown out of heaven and found herself on Wuthering Heights, the moors, and sobbed for joy.

Why won't she marry Heathcliff? Too degrading because he is poorly educated.

Who is listening and what is the listener's response? Heathcliff; he leaves.

What doesn't he hear Catherine say? That she loves him.

What does Catherine do when she realises who was listening? She searches for him in a storm, falls ill and convalesces at Thrushcross Grange.

What happens after that? The Linton parents die of the fever they caught from Catherine, and then three years later Catherine marries Edgar.

GCSE style question: how are Catherine's feelings represented in this chapter? As complicated; natural imagery is used to describe her feelings for both Heathcliff and Edgar.

Chapter 10

What happens after Catherine and Edgar have been married for six months? Heathcliff returns.

Why is Edgar surprised? Heathcliff is strong, handsome and seemingly well-educated.

Why is Edgar troubled by Catherine? He doesn't like the way she is attracted to Heathcliff.

What happens to Isabella? She becomes obsessed by Heathcliff.

Why is she annoyed with Catherine? She thinks Catherine is keeping

Heathcliff for herself.

What does Catherine do to get her own back on Isabella? She tells Heathcliff of Isabella's feelings.

What is Heathcliff's attitude towards Isabella? He doesn't like her, but is interested that she will inherit Edgar's property.

How does Nelly show her loyalty to Edgar? She tells him of Heathcliff's arrival.

What do you think happened to Heathcliff while he was away? Why does the author leave it a mystery, do you think? You should guess for this answer, but it is clear that he educates himself and makes money somehow.

Chapter 11

What does Hareton do to Nelly? He throws a stone at her.

What has Heathcliff taught Hareton to do? Swear at his father.

What does Nelly see Heathcliff doing with Isabella? Embracing her.

What does Heathcliff say when Catherine becomes angry with him? That she has treated him 'infernally' and that he is going to get his revenge.

Who tells Edgar what has happened? Nelly.

Why does Catherine lock Edgar and Heathcliff in a room? So that Edgar must face Heathcliff alone.

What happens to Edgar? He is humiliated by Heathcliff and then strikes him.

What does Catherine do when Edgar says she must decide him or Heathcliff? She has a fit and starves herself for three days.

What does Edgar threaten Isabella if she encourages Heathcliff? He will disown her.

GCSE style question: how is Nelly represented in this chapter? As siding with Edgar and disapproving of Catherine.

GCSE style question: how does Brontë create a sense of drama and conflict in the chapter? By having Catherine in the centre of a love triangle; by presenting Catherine as attractive, but unstable.

Chapter 12

How long does Catherine refuse food for? 3 days.

Why does Nelly not tell Edgar about her condition? Because she thinks Catherine is acting.

What does Catherine imagine in her delirium? That she is back at the Heights in the bed she shared with Heathcliff.

What does Catherine come to realise is the source of her misery? Being separated from the Heights and Heathcliff.

Why is Edgar angry with Nelly? For not telling him about how ill Catherine is.

What does Nelly hear about as she goes to fetch the doctor for Catherine? Of Isabella's elopement with Heathcliff.

Why doesn't she tell Edgar? She doesn't want to trouble him with the news.

What does Edgar do when he learns of the elopement? He disowns Isabella.

GCSE style question: how does Brontë present Nelly in this chapter? As very much part of the action in the way she deals with what she knows.

GCSE style question: how does Brontë present Catherine in this chapter? As someone who is gradually realizing what she has done to herself and the people around her.

Chapter 13

How long is Catherine ill for and with what? For two months with brain fever.

What does Isabella's letter reveal? That her marriage to Heathcliff was a mistake; that Heathcliff might be a devil; that Hareton threatened to set a dog on her when she tried to make friends with him; that Hindley wants to kill Heathcliff; that she is desperate for Nelly to visit.

GCSE style question: how does Brontë present Isabella in this chapter? As someone who has woken up to the nightmare that is Heathcliff and the Heights. She forms a counterpoint to Catherine who only realized that she loved the Heights when she lived at the Grange. With Isabella, it is the opposite.

Chapter 14

What does Edgar refuse to do? To write to Isabella.

What does Nelly find when she visits the Heights? That Isabella looks woebegone but Heathcliff looks very fine.

What does Heathcliff insist upon when he hears about Catherine's illness? That he visits her.

Why does Nelly come to agree to help Heathcliff see Catherine? Because he is so insistent; threatening to fight his way to her.

Why does Lockwood associate himself with Heathcliff and why is he presented in an ironic light? He believes he is like Heathcliff in his attraction to Cathy, Catherine's daughter, but shies away from her in case she is like her mother. We, the reader, realise he is nothing like Heathcliff because he lacks Heathcliff's passion.

GCSE style question: how is Heathcliff presented in this chapter? As revengeful and brutal; his poor treatment of Isabella is because he hates Edgar; as triumphant to a degree; he is proud of the victory he has achieved over Hindley; as passionate in his desperate desire to see Catherine.

Chapter 15

When does Nelly give Heathcliff's letter to Catherine? When Edgar is at church.

What does Heathcliff do? He bursts into the house before she gives an answer and takes her in his arms.

What does Heathcliff realise about Catherine? That she is going to die.

What does Catherine accuse Heathcliff of? Of killing her.

What does he accuse her of? Of breaking both their hearts by marrying Edgar.

How does their argument end? By both of them crying in each other's arms.

What does Heathcliff do when Edgar enters? He places Catherine's body in Edgar's arms.

GCSE style question: how does the author represent the desire to escape in this chapter? In many ways; there is a sense that both lovers want to be consumed by death.

GCSE style question: how does the author represent the themes of passion and betrayal in this chapter? We have a sense that Catherine and Heathcliff's love is too passionate to survive in the 'real' world.

Chapter 16

What happens to Catherine that night? Why? She dies giving birth.

When does Heathcliff realise what has happened to Catherine? Why? He realizes she is dead before Nelly tells him. He has a mystical connection to Catherine.

What does he hope Catherine will do? He hopes she will 'wake him in torment' and haunt him.

What does Heathcliff do to Catherine's locket? He replaces Edgar's hair with his own.

What does Nelly do? She gets Edgar's hair and entwines both men's hair with Catherine's.

Why is it convenient for Heathcliff that Edgar has no son? It means that the estate passes on to Isabella.

GCSE style question: how does the author present Heathcliff's trauma in this chapter? We see Heathcliff imagining that he is talking to the dead Catherine, saying, 'I cannot live without my life!'.

GCSE style question: why is Catherine's grave a fitting place for her? It borders the moor, which she loved to go to with Heathcliff.

Chapter 17

Where does Isabella return to after the funeral? Thrushcross Grange.

What do we learn from Isabella happened after the funeral when Heathcliff returned? Hindley locked the door, hoping to kill Heathcliff. Isabella warned Heathcliff, who grabbed Hindley's weapon, forced himself into Hindley's room and trampled him unconscious.

How and why did Heathcliff hurt Isabella? She taunted him about Catherine, and he threw a knife at her.

How did Isabella escape? She ran away as Heathcliff and Hindley were fighting.

Where does Isabella go and what happens to her? She goes to the South and gives birth to a son, Linton.

What happens six months after Catherine's death? Hindley dies.

What does Edgar try to do with Hareton? He tries to take him away from Heathcliff.

How does Heathcliff thwart Edgar's plans? Heathcliff threatens to take Linton away from Isabella.

How does Heathcliff come to own Wuthering Heights? He pays off Hindley's debts.

Who lives there as a servant? Hindley's son, Hareton.

How does the author use the pathetic fallacy in this chapter? The wintry weather after Catherine's death suggests the emotions of the characters.

GCSE style question: how and why is Heathcliff represented as brutal in this chapter? Isabella who is the narrator, doesn't like him, and represents his fight with Hindley as very brutal.

GCSE style question: how does Brontë develop the theme of revenge in this chapter? Isabella learns the need for revenge from Heathcliff; Heathcliff exacts his revenge on Hindley for Hindley's treatment of him when he was a child; Heathcliff plans to turn Hareton into a monster.

Chapter 18

What year/month does this chapter start in and how many years later is it? June 1797. 12 years later.

How is Catherine junior similar and different to her mother? She has her mother's energy, but she doesn't have her anger or fierce passion.

Why does Edgar visit Isabella? He hears she is dying and goes to visit her.

What does Cathy do? She escapes from the park on her pony.

Where does Nelly find her? At the Heights.

What does Nelly find out has happened? Cathy has met Hareton who has shown her Penistone Crags.

What does Cathy mistake Hareton for? For a servant.

How does she feel when learns Hareton is her cousin? Horrified.

What does Nelly persuade Cathy not to do? To tell Edgar of her visit.

GCSE style question: what do you think of the presentation of Cathy in this chapter? She is both similar and different to her mother; she has her energy, but not her spite.

Chapter 19

Who does Edgar bring back from London? What is he like? He returns with Isabella's son, Linton Heathcliff, who is sickly and babyish.

How does Cathy treat the new arrival? Like a pet.

What does Joseph arrive and say? He says that Linton must come to the Heights that night.

What is Edgar's response? He is very reluctant to let Linton go but he has no choice. He offers to bring Linton to the Heights the next morning as

Linton is sleeping.

How is Linton similar and different to Heathcliff? He is different in that he is very weak, but similar in the way he likes to dictate orders.

GCSE style question: what do you think of Brontë's representation of the second generation so far (Hareton, Cathy, Linton)? They share important similarities, but there are distinct differences too. Good answers will explore both.

Chapter 20

How does Nelly manage to get Linton to go to Heathcliff? She lies, giving excuses about the reasons why Heathcliff has not seen Linton, and saying that Heathcliff will be fonder than any uncle.

How does Heathcliff refer to Linton and Linton's mother when Linton arrives? As his "property" and Isabella as a "wicked slut".

Why does Heathcliff like the fact that Linton is here? He does not love him but likes the chance Linton will give him to have access to Thrushcross Grange.

What does Linton do as Nelly leaves? He pleads with her not to leave him there.

GCSE style question: how does Brontë represent Heathcliff and his son in this chapter? Heathcliff is represented as "mercenary" and wanting revenge. Linton is both unsympathetic and portrayed as a victim of circumstance.

Chapter 21

What does Cathy persuade Nelly to do on the anniversary of her mother's death? To take her to the moors.

Who do they meet there? Heathcliff.

What plan do we learn Heathcliff has? That Cathy and Linton should marry.

What happens when Cathy meets Linton and Hareton? Linton comes across as feeble (not being able to show Cathy around the house) so Hareton does instead. It becomes clear to Cathy that Hareton is very poorly educated, not being able to read his own name properly over the door.

What does Heathcliff confess about Hareton? That he could have loved him if he had not been Hindley's son and that he takes pleasure in how coarse and rude he is.

How does Cathy bond with Linton? Heathcliff sends Linton after his cousin, and they mock Hareton's inability to read.

How does Brontë build suspense in this chapter? Heathcliff's master plan for revenge appears to be coming to fruition.

What echoes are there in Linton's mocking of Hareton? Similar to Edgar's mocking Heathcliff in Chapter 7.

How is Linton's mockery of Hareton different from Edgar's mockery of Heathcliff? Linton is harsher and more deliberate, more vindictive.

Chapter 22

Why does Cathy not think of Linton much during the winter? Because she is nursing her father, who she thinks is dying.

What does the loss of Cathy's hat lead to? Meeting Heathcliff.

What does he tell Cathy off for? For not writing to Linton; for playing with Linton's heart.

What does he say about Linton? That he is dying of a broken heart for Cathy.

Why does Cathy go to Wuthering Heights? Because Heathcliff has made her feel guilty about Linton's state of mind and health.

How does Nelly's treatment of Cathy differ from her treatment of Catherine, her mother? Nelly more readily agrees to what Cathy wants because she likes her better, whereas she tended to torment Catherine because she found Catherine a difficult person (see Chapter 11 etc.).

Chapter 23

What is the weather like as Cathy and Nelly travel to Wuthering Heights? Raining.

Why does Cathy feel conflicted? She doesn't want to contradict her father by going to the Heights, but she feels guilty about Linton.

What does Linton complain about when they get there? The servants; Cathy for not visiting and then writing instead of visiting.

How does Cathy respond when Linton talks about love? She pushes his chair.

How does Linton deepen Cathy's guilty feelings? He has a coughing fit and says that she has made his condition worse, and that she needs to nurse him back to health as a result.

How does Cathy try to solve things? She nurses both Nelly, who has caught a fever, and her father during the day, and at night rides to the Heights to help Linton.

GCSE style question: how does Brontë explore the theme of guilt in chapters 22 and 23? She explores Cathy's conflicted feelings towards her father and Linton, showing how the people around her manipulate and persuade her to see the world from their point of view. A mother-child relationship develops between Cathy and Linton, who emotionally blackmails her.

Chapter 24

What does Cathy confess to Nelly? That she has been visiting the Heights and seeing Linton.

Why does Hareton become angry and what does he do as a result? Cathy makes fun of him for not knowing his numbers. Hareton forces Linton and Cathy into the kitchen.

Who does Linton blame for incident and why is he so upset? He blames Cathy. The incident made him cough blood.

How does Hareton try to apologise and why does his apology fail? He tries to stop Cathy's horse; she thinks he might be trying to murder her and whips him, galloping home.

What does Cathy learn to do with Linton later on in the chapter? She learns to endure his selfish behavior.

What does Edgar do when he learns of Cathy's visits to the Heights? He forbids her from going but says he will invite Linton to the Grange and she can write to him.

What does Nelly not tell Edgar and what is the result? She doesn't tell him how ill Linton is and this makes Edgar think that Cathy could have a secure marriage to Linton.

GCSE style question: how does Brontë develop Hareton's character in this chapter? She presents him as trapped by his own lack of education.

GCSE style question: how do we see Nelly developing as a character in this chapter? She has a pang of conscience and tells Edgar about the visits.

Chapter 25

Why does Nelly continue with her story? Because Lockwood begs her to continue.

What does Nelly Edgar about Linton? That he is in very poor health.

What does Edgar eventually concede? That if Cathy would be happy marrying Linton then he will agree to it, even though he knows Heathcliff will have got what he wants.

Where does Edgar agree Cathy can meet Linton and what condition? On the moors under Nelly's supervision.

GCSE style question: how is Edgar presented in this chapter and the rest of the book? He is presented as misguided; he wanted to help Catherine and Cathy, but he never manages to help because he offers poor advice. He is presented, to a certain degree, as a tragic figure; he wants to do the right thing but never can.

Chapter 26

Why is Linton not at the agreed place? Because Heathcliff wants to lure Cathy much nearer to the Heights.

Why is Linton's health an issue? Linton insists that he is getting better, but Cathy and Nelly feel he seems very ill.

What is Linton's mood? He seems scared, constantly looking back at the Heights.

What does Linton extract from Cathy? A promise to meet him next Thursday.

What do Cathy and Nelly discuss? Linton's health and that they will work how ill he is next meeting.

GCSE style question: how is Linton presented differently in this chapter? He seems much more scared, and more romantic.

Chapter 27

Who is dying? Edgar.

Why does Cathy go with Nelly and meet Linton? Because she promised to.

What is Linton terrified about? He is terrified that he will be killed if Cathy leaves him.

Who appears and what does he persuade Cathy and Nelly to do? Heathcliff appears and persuades Nelly and Cathy to help Linton back to the Heights.

What happens to Nelly and Cathy at the Heights? Heathcliff imprisons them at the Heights; he beats Cathy for trying to get the key to the door.

What does Linton tell them when Heathcliff goes for horses? That his father wants them to marry the next day.

On what condition does Cathy say she will marry Linton? If Heathcliff allows her to see her father.

What is Heathcliff's response? He says he will like to see Edgar so unhappy, and will not set her free until after she is married.

GCSE style question: how does Brontë suggest that Cathy is like her mother in this chapter? By the way she stands up to Heathcliff with 'her black eyes flashing with passion'.

GCSE style question: how does Brontë suggest Linton's selfishness? By the way he is upset that her tears have spoilt his cup after Heathcliff beats Cathy; by the way he appears to enjoy other people's pain.

Chapter 28

Who releases Nelly and when? Zillah, the housekeeper after six days.

What does Linton tell Nelly? That Cathy is still a prisoner and all her property, her books included, belongs to him. He tells her that Heathcliff hit her and crushed her father's portrait which was in a locket, which Linton had wanted for himself.

How does Heathcliff manage to stop Edgar making sure Linton won't get Cathy's property? He has bribed the lawyer to delay things so that the contract which will ensure Cathy's property is protected is never drawn up.

How does Cathy manage to comfort her father before he dies? She escapes from the Heights and is with Edgar when he dies.

Who does Edgar feel convinced he will join in death? Catherine, Cathy's mother.

Who is now in control? Heathcliff now is in control of the Grange and the Heights because the husband has control of his wife's property, according to the legal system of the time.

GCSE style question: how does Brontë explore the theme of violence in this chapter? Linton vividly describes the way Heathcliff hurts Cathy, her mouth 'filling with blood'.

Chapter 29

Why has Heathcliff punished Linton? For his role in helping Cathy to escape.

Why does Heathcliff refuse to let Cathy live at the Grange? She has to work for her keep at the Heights.

Why does Cathy have to obey Heathcliff and Linton? They have better legal claims to the Grange than Cathy because of the patriarchal legal system.

How does Cathy stand up to Heathcliff? She says she loves Linton and that Heathcliff is alone in the world.

What does Heathcliff confess to Nelly as Cathy packs her things? That he believes in ghosts and particularly the ghost of Catherine, which he has seen and felt.

What does Heathcliff instruct Nelly not to do? Visit the Heights.

GCSE style question: how does Brontë make Heathcliff a complex character in this chapter and at other parts in the novel? We feel sympathy for him when he talks about seeing Catherine's ghost. He comes across as a Romantic, believing in eternal love. Yet, his treatment of Linton, Cathy and Nelly is despicable. But we understand, within the context of the novel, why he is behaving this way.

Chapter 30

Who now gives us information about Cathy? Zillah, the housekeeper.

Why do Zillah and Hareton not help Cathy? Because Heathcliff had ordered Zillah and Hareton not to help Cathy.

Who looks exclusively after Linton until he dies? Cathy.

How does Cathy behave after his death and why? She refuses to let Hareton or Zillah to be nice to her because of the way they behaved when her father died.

What does Lockwood tell Nelly? That Heathcliff could look for another tenant for the Grange.

What evidence is there that there is an attraction between Hareton and Cathy? Hareton offers her a seat by the fire and food and Cathy permits him to get her books back for her, which are out of reach.

Why does Heathcliff want to stop any romance between Hareton and Cathy? Because of the way Hareton's father, Hindley, treated him and because he is miserable, he doesn't want anyone else to be happy.

GCSE style question: how does this chapter make the story come full circle? We are back to the time when Lockwood first visited the Grange with the end of Zillah's story.

Chapter 31

Why can't Cathy respond to Nelly's letter? Because she has no paper; Heathcliff has deprived her of it.

How does Cathy humiliate Hareton? Because he is unable to read Nelly's letter.

How does Hareton respond? He hits her and throws her books into the fire.

What does Lockwood overhear Heathcliff saying about Hareton? How his face reminds him of Catherine.

What does Lockwood realise as he rides back to the Grange? That he did the right thing in not following Nelly's wishes and striking up a romance with Cathy.

How do we see Heathcliff changing in this chapter? His heart seems to be softening; he seems less intent upon revenge.

GCSE style question: what do you think of Brontë's presentation of Cathy and Hareton? She subtly presents their growing friendship.

Chapter 32

When does Lockwood visit the Grange again? How much time has passed since he was at the Grange? He visits in September 1802, having left in January 1802, therefore roughly seven months have passed.

Where has Nelly moved to? The Heights.

How are things different? The atmosphere is much happier both in the surroundings and the people; there are flowers and fruit on the trees.

How is Cathy helping Hareton? She is helping him to read.

Why does Lockwood feel envious? He sees how Hareton and Cathy like each other.

Why is Joseph disgusted? He thinks Cathy has bewitched Hareton.

What news does Nelly give Lockwood? That Heathcliff died in May and that Hareton and Cathy have become lovers.

How is the story between Hareton and Cathy similar to Beauty and the Beast? Hareton is like the beast who Cathy has tamed and made human.

How have books brought Hareton and Cathy together? She has taught him to read; they have 'civilized' him.

Chapter 33

What do Hareton and Cathy do to Joseph's blackcurrant bushes? They replace them with flowers.

What is Cathy's response when Joseph complains? That Heathcliff can't complain because he stole all her and Hareton's property.

What does Heathcliff do when he learns that she has said this? He attacks her and then lets her go, observing her face.

What does Heathcliff feel Cathy's face looks like? Catherine's, her mother's.

What does he tell Cathy about his desire for revenge? That it is gone.

What does he confess? That he feels very lonely and that Hareton and Cathy remind him of Catherine. He feels a change coming on.

What does he become obsessed by? Joining Catherine.

GCSE style question: how does Brontë present Heathcliff in this chapter?

As much more sympathetic than before; as poetic in his desire to return to Catherine.

Chapter 34

What do Hareton and Cathy do in the nice April weather? Garden.

What does Heathcliff do? He isolates himself, starving himself for four days.

How does he die? He tells Nelly that he is 'within sight of my heaven'. He won't see a doctor or minister, despite Nelly urging him to. Nelly finds him dead with the window open.

Where is he buried and who comes to the funeral? He is buried next to Catherine. Hareton is the only mourner.

What have the local people seen? The ghosts of Heathcliff and Cathy together.

What does Lockwood see before he leaves the area and what does he imagine? Why is the ending possibly ironic? The peaceful scene of Edgar, Catherine and Heathcliff's graves. He imagines that they are all at peace. The reader may feel that they are not at peace, particularly given what the locals say about Heathcliff and Catherine's ghosts.

GCSE style question: how does Brontë make the death of Heathcliff so compelling and poignant? During both Catherine and Heathcliff's death scenes, a 'beck' makes a sound, suggesting a connection between them. Heathcliff has given up on revenge; he has lost the nastiness that made him so unsympathetic in the latter half of the novel.

Speaking and Listening Exercises

Work in a group and devise a **chatshow** based on the novel. Make sure that you have an interviewer (chat-show host) who questions the main characters in the novel about their thoughts and feelings regarding what has happened to them. The aim is that students need to show that they understand the storyline and characters by talking in role about the events in the novel. You can include dead characters such as Catherine, Heathcliff, Edgar, old Earnshaw, Hindley, Isabella, and Linton.

You could put Heathcliff on **trial** for his crimes: imprisoning Isabella, imprisoning Catherine and forcing her into marrying Linton. Set things up so that you have a prosecuting lawyer who is accusing him of his various crimes. Have a defence lawyer who argues that Heathcliff is not guilty. Call witnesses for the prosecution and defence who are characters from the novel or the author. You can be deliberately "loose" with your approach and have "dead" characters appear. You could have Hindley, his wife Frances, Edgar, Nelly, Isabella, Cathy called for the prosecution, and possibly Catherine, old Earnshaw, Hareton in defence. Use the trial to explore different views on the novel. Then possibly write it up as a script or review what you have learnt from doing it.

Put the main characters in **therapy**. Have them visit a therapist to discuss their problems with him/her. You could do this so that they go into therapy at various stages during the novel, i.e. Heathcliff/Catherine or Hareton/Cathy talking about things at the different phases of the novel; after the time when Heathcliff leaves, his return, Catherine's death, the imprisoning of Isabella, the marriage between Linton and Cathy, Hareton and Cathy's growing attachment. Write a review of what you have learnt from doing this afterwards.

Work in a group and devise a **radio drama** of the major parts of the novel. Different groups could work on different sections of the book; e.g. Lockwood's arrival, Heathcliff's childhood, his disappearance, Catherine being torn between Edgar and Heathcliff, Catherine's death, Cathy's marriage to Linton, Heathcliff's death. Make the drama short and punchy. This exercise will help you get to know the text in much more depth: the editing of the novel will help you summarise key points.

How to write top grade essays on the novel

In order to write a good essay about *Wuthering Heights*, you need to understand it. You will need to know what the difficult vocabulary means and be aware of how the text is the product of the world it comes from: early Victorian England. You will also need to be aware of what the examiners for your particular question are looking for. For GCSE, it appears that most questions are, at the time of writing this guide, "extract based"; you will be given a small extract and asked to consider how the author builds suspense or drama in the extract, or presents the characters or key themes in a particular way. In order to achieve highly, you will need to answer the question carefully and not simply re-tell the extract; this is something that I have seen many good students do. The A Level questions on *Wuthering Heights* are much more like the ones posed in the **essay question section** of this study guide and the A Level style questions posed at the end of the chapter questions. Sometimes, you might be asked to compare the novel with other literary texts, depending upon the nature of the task and/or exam board. For A Level, you need to be aware of other literary critics' views on the novel.

You should consider a few key questions:

For extract questions, consider how has the author **built up** to this particular moment? Think carefully about what the reader already knows before they have read the extract. You will need to know the story well in order to do this.

What literary devices does the author use to make the passage interesting or to reveal a particular character in a certain light? Think very carefully about the author's use of language: Brontë's use of descriptions to create a certain atmosphere or paint a sketch of a character/event; her use of dialogue to reveal character and create drama/tension; her use of imagery (metaphors/similes/personification). You will need to pack your essay full of the relevant terminology if you want to aim for higher marks as it appears many mark schemes as a key requirement.

You need to be aware of a number of different interpretations of the novel. The weblinks below should help you with this.

Finally, you need to provide evidence and analysis to back up your points. As a cornerstone of your essay writing technique, you should be aware of the **PEEL** method of analysing texts: making a Point, providing Evidence, Explaining how your evidence endorses your point, and Linking to a new point.

Writing about the story/narrative

I would strongly advise you to read my section on the **structure and themes of the novel here** before writing about the effects the narrative structure of the book creates. There are many, many things to say about the story of the book, but you should think about your own personal response as well: what did you find the most engaging parts of the novel and why? Look back over the notes you have made while you read the novel and use them to shape an original response. You need to avoid just re-telling the story, which is very easy to do in highly pressurised situations and you're not thinking straight!

Writing about the characterisations

There are many websites which can help you with writing about the characters in the novel, including the **The Reader's Guide to Wuthering Heights website here**. What most of them don't say is a very important thing I've already mentioned; Brontë's characters are *not* real people, they are literary creations and we become interested in them because of their similarities and differences. A central technique of Brontë's is to make the reader think about how and why characters are similar and different; we are constantly being invited to compare and contrast characters in our minds. This is a central way that Brontë's generates suspense and drama in the novel; the novel is full striking comparisons and contrasts. Where Heathcliff is passionate, impulsive, powerful and horribly discriminated against at the beginning of the novel, Edgar Linton is privileged, vacillating, and inherently but not horribly snobbish. Heathcliff and Edgar are both similar and different: they both love Catherine desperately, but the nature of their loves are very different in quality and intensity. Heathcliff and Catherine are interesting to compare and contrast as well; they share a love of the moors, a love of each other, and are both very passionate. But Catherine's social position sets her apart from the 'low-born' Heathcliff. There are important similarities and differences between Catherine and her daughter, Cathy as well. Indeed, most characters in the book have strong points of connection and contrast with other characters in the book. This is a central technique of Brontë's; to make us constantly think about how and why the characters are similar and different.

Task

Look at some character studies online, such as **the Shmoop one,** and devise a chart or **visual organiser** which illustrates the similarities and differences between the major characters, exploring the effects that these similarities and differences have upon the reader.

As has been mentioned, the British Library has a good website:
http://www.bl.uk/romantics-and-victorians/videos/wuthering-heights-who-is-heathcliff

The BBC Bitesize website also has some useful points:
http://www.bbc.co.uk/schools/gcsebitesize/english_literature/prosewutheringheights/wutheringheights_character/revision/1/

Writing about the settings

Emily Brontë is an interesting writer because she shares a Romantic artist's love of nature and describing nature. In the novel, natural settings play a very important part of the book. Equally, domestic settings such as the houses at Thrushcross Grange and Wuthering Heights play very important roles too: these two places have both symbolic and metaphorical meanings.

You can find more information about settings here:
http://www.shmoop.com/wuthering-heights/setting.html

This Slideshow on Slideshare has many useful quotes and exercises regarding settings:
http://www.slideshare.net/jcbrignell/place-and-setting-in-wuthering-heights

There is an excellent webpage on the British Library website devoted to the novel here:

http://www.bl.uk/romantics-and-victorians/articles/walking-the-landscape-of-wuthering-heights

Task

Look carefully at the use of settings in the novel; what purpose do they serve? Why does Brontë set particular scenes in particular settings?

Passion

As I have already said, a central technique of Brontë's is to make the reader feel extreme emotions; the novel is supposed to be passionate! Once you begin to appreciate the passion of the novel and understand how Brontë creates such passionate characters such as Heathcliff and Catherine, you will be in a better place to analyse the novel. A central technique which creates passion is her use of various literary techniques to create an emotional response. An important device is the use of dramatic irony; this is when we know more information than one or more of the characters know. Dramatic irony is used in this novel repeatedly through the deployment of multiple narrators and manipulating time. The voices of Lockwood, Nelly, Catherine, Heathcliff, Isabella and Cathy constantly give us new perspectives on the various situations; each person is, in their own way, an unreliable narrator. This creates irony throughout the novel; we, the reader, nearly always know more than the person telling the story does about certain issues. Above all, the reader is constantly asking him/herself: what is the nature of the passion that the characters have for each other? For example, Heathcliff and Edgar's passion for Catherine; Linton, Lockwood and Hareton's love for Cathy. The different temporal and narrative perspectives give us a continuously changing picture of the nature of the passion the characters feel for each other.

This website is probably the best on points of view:

http://academic.brooklyn.cuny.edu/english/melani/novel_19c/wuthering/narrator.html

Task

Look back over the novel, and work out what the passionate parts of the novel are and why they are passionate. Devise a visual organiser which charts the passionate moments so that you can see clearly on one page where such moments occur, and think about the effect they have upon the reader.

Use of language

Above all, you need to explore the effects of Brontë's language upon the reader; exploring what the language makes the reader think, feel and see.

These websites contain some incisive analysis on the use of language.

The BBC Bitesize website is a good place to start:
http://www.bbc.co.uk/schools/gcsebitesize/english_literature /prosewutheringheights/wutheringheights_language/revision/1 /

There is an excellent essay on speech in *Wuthering Heights* here:
http://campuses.fortbendisd.com/campuses/documents/teach er/2009%5Cteacher_20090122_1237.pdf

The most academic document about language in *WH* that can be freely accessed on the web is here:
http://iosrjournals.org/iosr-jhss/papers/Vol2-issue5/H0254650.pdf?id=5681

Task

Devise a chart/visual organiser/notes on the different types of language Brontë uses in the novel, providing quotes and examples for the following types of language:

Descriptive language: language which describes people, places and situations

Imagery: language which makes comparisons

Important dialogue: important quotes that people say that make the plot move on.

Useful links

The Shmoop section on literary devices is useful but don't copy it blindly. Read it through and look at the other sites such as Sparknotes/Cliffnotes etc, and come to your own judgements about you think are the important points:
http://www.shmoop.com/wuthering-heights/literary-devices.html

There is a set of interactive flashcards on the literary devices to be found here:
https://quizlet.com/59296027/wuthering-height-literary-terms-flash-cards/

Personally, I think the British Library contains the best resources for *Wuthering Heights* on the web, with a wealth of original manuscripts, reviews and videos to look at. A good place to start is here, with an early review of the novel:
http://www.bl.uk/works/wuthering-heights

Possible essay titles

Is *Wuthering Heights* a novel more about love or hate? Discuss.

'Heathcliff is too brutal in the novel ever to be sympathetic.' To what extent do you agree with this statement?

To what extent is *Wuthering Heights* a novel about the oppression of women?

What role does social class play in the novel?

How and why do the settings play such an important role in the novel?

Analyse and explore the role dialect plays in the novel.

Glossary

Co dependency Unhelpful and poor behaviour learned by family members to survive in an emotionally painful and stressful environment which causes pain itself

Conveyed Showed

Degraded Debased, lowered in value

Diabolical Devilish

Genre Type of text, e.g. horror, western

Gothic An adjective describing narratives which are full of supernatural happenings and extreme emotions, involving damsels in distress in haunted castles

Dramatisation Presenting in a dramatic way

Imagery All the poetic devices in a text, in particular the visual images created for the reader's mind to feed on and the comparisons that make a reader think and reflect upon an issue

Impregnable Unbeatable

Irony A literary device where the author doesn't mean fully what they are saying, where there are other meanings behind the literal one

Melodrama A story with extreme emotional events and characters, e.g. suicides, threats, blackmail, mad wives, lustful husbands

Misanthropist A person who hates company, wants to be alone

Passively aggressive Behaviour which is aimed at causing pain and upset but appears to be innocent, where the person who is being aggressive looks as if they are passive, or not doing anything

Pathos A literary device which makes the reader feel sorry for a character

Poignant Moving, emotional
Prevail Overcome
Psychoanalytical parable A story which has a message about human nature
Pseudonymously Under a different name
Omniscient All knowing
Social status A person's position in society
Subservient Slavish
Tempestuous Stormy
Theme An important idea in a text
Tone An atmosphere conveyed in the writing
Vicissitudes a variation in circumstances or fortune at different times in your life or in the development of something;
Victorian Belonging to the UK's Victorian era (i.e. the reign of Queen Victoria, 1837–1901)

About the Author

Francis Gilbert is a Lecturer in Education at Goldsmiths, University of London, teaching on the PGCE Secondary English programme and the MA in Children's Literature with Professor Michael Rosen. Previously, he worked for a quarter of a century in various English state schools teaching English and Media Studies to 11-18 year olds. He has also moonlighted as a journalist, novelist and social commentator both in the UK and international media. He is the author of *Teacher On The Run*, *Yob Nation*, *Parent Power*, *Working The System -- How To Get The Very Best State Education for Your Child*, and a novel about school, *The Last Day Of Term*. His first book, *I'm A Teacher, Get Me Out Of Here* was a big hit, becoming a bestseller and being serialised on Radio 4. In his role as an English teacher, he has taught many classic texts over the years and has developed a great many resources to assist readers with understanding, appreciating and responding to them both analytically and creatively. This led him to set up his own small publishing company FGI Publishing (fgipublishing.com) which has published his study guides as well as a number of books by other authors, including Roger Titcombe's *Learning Matters* and Tim Cadman's *The Changes*.

He is the co-founder, with Melissa Benn and Fiona Millar, of The Local Schools Network, **www.localschoolsnetwork.org.uk**, a blog that celebrates non-selective state schools, and also has his own website, **www.francisgilbert.co.uk** and a Mumsnet blog, **www.talesbehindtheclassroomdoor.co.uk**.

He has appeared numerous times on radio and TV, including Newsnight, the Today Programme, Woman's Hour and the Russell Brand Show. In June 2015, he was awarded a PhD in Creative Writing and Education by the University of London.

Printed in Great Britain
by Amazon

69302300R00059